Being Conservative from A to Z

An Anthology and Guide
for Busy Conservative-Minded People

S.R. Piccoli

DEDICATION

*

This book
is dedicated to all
those who looked for truth
in politics in all the wrong places.
I hope they find out what was wrong
in their previous search attempts. Otherwise,
I wish them all the luck in the world—they'll need it.

CONTENTS

BEING CONSERVATIVE FROM A TO Z

ACKNOWLEDGMENTS

"God keep me from ever completing anything.
This whole book is but a draught—nay, but a draught of a draught.
Oh, Time, Strength, Cash, and Patience."
(Herman Melville, *Moby Dick*)

I wish to thank all those—too many to mention individually—who
taught me the art of thinking, without which this book
would never have been written.
I also wish to thank my good friend Peter Weevers,
who revised my English text and also made suggestions
to make it sound better to native speakers

INTRODUCTION

As a good detective would say, the more you ask the right questions the more likely you are to get the right answers— and the less time you waste. From this point of view the best option would be to avoid questions that are too direct, because direct interrogation requires simple and straightforward answers, which is what is lacking in today's complicated and often confusing world. In the case in point here, the best way to begin our investigation wouldn't sound like this: What does it mean to be a Conservative? This is even truer if we narrow the focus to the American political tradition. In fact, American conservatism has always embraced elements of classical liberalism, and this to the extent that it would be reasonable to advance that the ideas of classical liberalism are the core of modern conservatism in America. But, as we know, liberalism has its roots in Enlightenment, while conservatism has its roots in the critique of Enlightenment...

As if that weren't enough, things get even more complicated if we embrace the point of view of English philosopher Michael Oakeshott on being conservative: "My theme is not a creed or a doctrine, but a disposition. To be conservative is to be disposed to think and behave in certain manners; it is to prefer certain kinds of conduct and certain conditions of human circumstances to others; it is to be disposed to make certain kinds of choices…"

However, although debatable in many respects, Oakeshott's definition of conservatism as a disposition rather than a belief from general principles is food for thought. Firstly, as a new kind of approach, it's intellectually challenging and stimulating—more concrete, and therefore more understandable—to a complex and multi-faceted political philosophy. Secondly, it is pedagogically useful because it seems to automatically provide an abundant amount of information on a very wide variety of topics that are directly or closely related to the main subject. By the way, that's the method used in this book. By looking through its pages one can easily perceive the operational scheme which consists of (implicitly) asking and answering questions such as "What does a conservative feel and think about this or that issue/topic/event?"

Michael Oakeshott's above-quoted statement is from a lecture delivered at Swansea University, U.K., in 1956[1], but a similar sentiment was echoed almost forty years later by Russell Kirk in *The Politics of Prudence*:[2]

> Being neither a religion nor an ideology, the body of opinion termed *conservatism* possesses no Holy Writ and no *Das Kapital* to provide dogmata. So far as it is possible to determine what conservatives believe, the first principles of the conservative persuasion are derived from what leading conservative writers and public men have professed during the past two centuries. [...]
>
> Perhaps it would be well, most of the time, to use this word "conservative" as an adjective chiefly. For there exists no Model Conservative, and conservatism is the negation of ideology: it is a state of mind, a type of character, a way of looking at the civil social order.

The attitude we call conservatism is sustained by a body of sentiments, rather than by a system of ideological dogmata. It is almost true that a conservative may be defined as a person who thinks himself such. The conservative movement or body of opinion can accommodate a considerable diversity of views on a good many subjects, there being no Test Act or Thirty-Nine Articles of the conservative creed.

In its own way, this book reflects the above-described approach, since "by default" it refers to what important leading conservative thinkers and public men have professed during the past two centuries up until the present time, no matter how many or how big the differences between the various thinkers on many issues might be.

That being said, however, as Russell Kirk himself points out, there is a great line of demarcation in modern politics: on one side of that line are those who think that the temporal order is the only order, and in consequence material needs are the only needs, on the other side are those who "recognize an enduring moral order in the universe" and "a constant human nature." As Eric Vogelin put it, the fundamental source of order in history and society is rooted in experiences of transcendence, in the attunement to divine reality. In other words, and as Voegelin himself would put it, the line of demarcation is between those who think that religious experience is the ground of political order and those who don't. That is where we must start. And as a matter of fact, this is how Russell Kirk's famous list of ten conservative principles[3] begins: "First, the conservative believes that there exists an enduring moral order. That order is made for man, and man is made for it: human nature is a constant, and moral truths are permanent." The rest of the list—widely regarded as perhaps the best general definition of "conservative"—is interesting as well. Here is a summary (titles & a few explanatory remarks when necessary):

- *"Second, conservative adheres to custom, convention, and continuity"* (*conservatives prefer the devil they know to the devil they don't know*).
- *"Third, conservatives believe in what may be called the principle of prescription"* (*that is, "things established by immemorial usage"*).
- *"Forth, conservatives are guided by their principle of prudence"* (*in the statesman, prudence is a chief virtue*).
- *"Fifth, conservatives pay attention to the principle of variety"* (*different is beautiful, God bless variety... "the only true forms of equality are equality at the Last Judgment and equality before a just court of law"*).
- *"Sixth, conservatives are chastened by their principle of imperfectability"* (*conservatives believe that there is a universal human nature, and that this nature is imperfect... but if man is imperfect, no perfect social order ever can be created*).
- *"Seventh, conservatives are persuaded that freedom and property are closely linked"* (*great civilizations are built upon the foundation of private property*).
- *"Eighth, conservatives uphold voluntary community, quite as they oppose involuntary collectivism."*
- *"Ninth, the conservative perceives the need for prudent restraints upon power and upon human passions"* (*conservatives endeavor to arrange government and society in such a way to avoid anarchy and tyranny*).
- *"Tenth, the thinking conservative understands that permanence and change must be recognized and reconciled in a vigorous society."*

This book, which could be described as an anthology of conservative analysis and insights on some key issues, is for readers who wish to acquaint themselves with conservative political thought and to get a critical and comparative perspective on what passes for political, social, economic, and cultural conservatism in their own time and place.

The book is intended for both European and American readers. It provides readings from European and American thinkers, which besides may help to call attention to some of the peculiarities of American conservatives, who, for instance, believe in Progress even more than liberals do. Last but not least, as the subtitle reads, this volume wants to be a teaching tool and a guide "for busy conservative-minded people," even though I must confess that I don't know what "busy people"—whether conservative-minded or not—exactly means...

Be it as it may, despite its brevity and modesty, I hope this book, will lead readers to a greater appreciation of conservative values and principles. After all, as we all know, the ways of the Lord are mysterious.

---

1   Michael Oakeshott, "On Being Conservative" in *Rationalism in Politics*, London: Methuen and Co. Ltd, 1962, p.168.

2   Russell Kirk, "Ten Conservative Principles" (originally a lecture given at The Heritage Foundation, March 20, 1986) in his *The Politics of Prudence*, Wilmington, Delaware: ISI Books, 1993, p. 15.

3   *Ibid.*, p. 17.

1

Ⓐ AMERICAN REVOLUTION

By and large, the American Revolution was not an innovating upheaval, but a conservative restoration of colonial prerogatives. Accustomed from their beginnings to self-government, the colonials felt that by inheritance they possessed the rights of Englishmen and by prescription certain rights peculiar to themselves. When a designing king and a distant parliament presumed to extend over America powers of taxation and administration never before exercised, the colonies rose to vindicate their prescriptive freedom; and after the hour for compromise had slipped away, it was with reluctance and trepidation they declared their independence. Thus men essentially conservative found themselves triumphant rebels, and were compelled to reconcile their traditional ideas with the necessities of an independence hardly anticipated.

~*Russell Kirk* [1]

Thomas Jefferson once said that, "every man has two countries—his own and France." Today, one could advance that, every man has two countries—his own and America. That's why U.S. history, from the American

Revolution to the present day, matters to everyone, everywhere. This is even truer for those who value conservatism or seek to understand it. Edmund Burke's insight into the conservative dynamic at the heart of the American Revolution is, from this point of view, a fundamental landmark in understanding the nature of that major historical event.

Unlike the French Revolution, which was a destructive and chaotic break between past and present, the American experience was limited, and aimed at allowing Americans the benefits derived from the experiences of the English. This to the point that the U.S. Constitution was seen by the Founding Fathers and by the American people as an extension of the ideas of Magna Carta and the English Bill of Rights.

In other words—and this is what matters most here—Burke's insight into the originally conservative nature of the American Revolution admonishes that, "however much some of us may wish the cherishing of liberty to be found in company with the advocacy of progressive causes, they are much more likely to be antagonists than allies."[2]

Here are a couple of excerpts, both of which are as insightful as they are self-explanatory, and therefore do not call for further comments. The first[3] is from Burke's "Speech on Moving Resolutions for Conciliation with America," the latter[4] is from Roger Scruton's *Culture Counts: Faith and Feeling in a World Besieged.*

> In this character of the Americans a love of freedom is the predominating feature which marks and distinguishes the whole: and as an ardent is always a jealous affection, your colonies become suspicious, restive, and untractable, whenever they see the least attempt to wrest from them by force, or shuffle from them by chicane, what they think the only advantage worth living for. This fierce spirit of liberty is stronger in the English

colonies, probably, than in any other people of the earth, and this from a great variety of powerful causes; which, to understand the true temper of their minds, and the direction which this spirit takes, it will not be amiss to lay open somewhat more largely.

First, the people of the colonies are descendants of Englishmen. England, Sir, is a nation which still, I hope, respects, and formerly adored, her freedom. The colonists emigrated from you when this part of your character was most predominant; and they took this bias and direction the moment they parted from your hands. They are therefore not only devoted to liberty, but to liberty according to English ideas and on English principles. Abstract liberty, like other mere abstractions, is not to be found. Liberty inheres in some sensible object; and every nation has formed to itself some favorite point, which by way of eminence becomes the criterion of their happiness. It happened, you know, Sir, that the great contests for freedom in this country were from the earliest times chiefly upon the question of taxing. Most of the contests in the ancient commonwealths turned primarily on the right of election of magistrates, or on the balance among the several orders of the state. The question of money was not with them so immediate. But in England it was otherwise. On this point of taxes the ablest pens and most eloquent tongues have been exercised, the greatest spirits have acted and suffered. In order to give the fullest satisfaction concerning the importance of this point, it was not only necessary for those who in argument defended the excellence of the English Constitution to insist on this privilege of granting money as a dry point of fact, and to prove that the right had been acknowledged in ancient parchments and blind usages to reside in a certain body called an House of Commons: they went much further: they attempted to prove, and they succeeded, that in theory it ought to be so, from the particular nature of a House of Commons, as an immediate representative of the people, whether the old records had delivered this oracle or not. They took infinite pains to inculcate, as a fundamental principle, that in all monarchies the people must in effect themselves, mediately or immediately, possess the power of granting their own money, or no shadow of liberty could subsist.

The colonies draw from you, as with their life-blood, these ideas and principles. Their love of liberty, as with you, fixed and attached on this specific point of taxing. Liberty might be safe or might be endangered in twenty other particulars without their being much pleased or alarmed. Here they felt its pulse; and as they found that beat, they thought themselves sick or sound. I do not say whether they were right or wrong in applying your general arguments to their own case. It is not easy, indeed, to make a monopoly of theorems and corollaries. The fact is, that they did thus apply those general arguments; and your mode of governing them, whether through lenity or indolence, through wisdom or mistake, confirmed them in the imagination, that they, as well as you, had an interest in these common principles.

~Edmund Burke

It is because of America, its success, its conflicts, and its symbolic importance in the world, that the question raised by Spengler is still with us: the question of Western identity. Take away America, its freedom, its optimism, its institutions, its Judeo-Christian beliefs, and its educational tradition, and little would remain of the West, besides the geriatric routines of a now toothless Europe. Add America to the discussion, and all the dire prophecies and mournful valedictions of the twentieth century seem faintly ridiculous. Yet, precisely because the West now depends upon America, a country launched on a path that recognizes no place and no time as its own, Western identity has become an urgent matter of debate. [...]

Our civilization has been uprooted. But when a tree is uprooted it does not always die. Sap may find its way to the branches, which break into leaf each spring with the perennial hope of living things. Such is our condition, and it is for this reason that culture has become not just precious to us, but a genuine political cause, the primary way of conserving our moral heritage and of standing firm in the face of a clouded future.

At the same time, the decline in religious faith means that many people, both skeptics and vacillators, begin to repudiate their cultural inheritance. [...] Our educational institutions offer privileged positions to those who disparage the old values, old hierarchies and old forms of social order that lie hidden in the curriculum that has come down to us. There is nothing to teach in the name of culture, they tell us, except the prejudices of other ages. [...]

Paradoxically, this new relativism, which has invaded every area of the humanities, goes hand in hand with an equally obstinate censoriousness. Many teachers are angry at the traditional works of our culture, and seek either to remove them from the curriculum or to hedge them around with prohibitions, seeing them as mere survivals of patriarchal, aristocratic, bourgeois, or theocratic attitudes that no longer have a claim on us. This posture of skepticism towards the classics displays a profound misjudgment. For the great works of Western culture are remarkable for the distance that they maintained from the norms and orthodoxies that gave birth to them. Only a very shallow reading of Chaucer or Shakespeare would see those writers as endorsing the societies in which they lived, or would overlook the far more important fact that their works hold mankind to the light of moral judgment, and examine, with all the love and all the pity that it calls for, the frailty of human nature. It is precisely the aspiration towards universal truth, towards a God's-eye perspective on the human condition, that is the hallmark of Western culture. And it is for that reason that we should see the American Revolution, rather than the French, as the turning point in our history, the moment when Western civilization became identical to the modern world—for that was the moment when Enlightenment took power.

~Roger Scruton

1. Russell Kirk, *The Conservative Mind: From Burke to Eliot*, Washington, DC: Regnery Publishing, Inc., 2001, p. 72.
2. David Womersley, 'Introduction'*Liberty and American Experience in the Eighteenth Century*, Indianapolis: Liberty Fund., 2006, p.20.
3. Edmund Burke, "Speech on Moving Resolutions for Conciliation with America," in *Works of the Right Honourable Edmund Burke* ,vol. II (of 12), London: John C. Nimmo, 1887, pp.120-122.
4. Roger Scruton, 'Preface'*Culture Counts: Faith and Feeling in a World Besieged*, New York: Encounter Books, 2007, vii-xiv.

2

ℬ BIGOTRY (FROM ATHEISTS)

Bigotry means, in common acceptation, an excessive or obstinate adherence to things or persons, to principles or party, *against* reason or *without* reason. The Oxford English Dictionary defines bigotry as, "obstinate or unenlightened attachment to a particular creed, opinion, system or party." Yet the first association that comes to mind is the religious one, and therefore bigotry is more often interpreted as "religious bigotry." Few seem to know that there is also an anti-religious bigotry, and most of those few are conservatives…

> The literary cabal had some years ago formed something like a regular plan for the destruction of the Christian religion. This object they pursued with a degree of zeal which hitherto had been discovered only in the propagators of some system of piety. They were possessed with a spirit of proselytism in the most fanatical degree; and from thence, by an easy progress, with the spirit of persecution according to their means. What was not to be done towards their great end by any direct or immediate act, might be wrought by a longer process through the medium of opinion. To

command that opinion, the first step is to establish a dominion over those who direct it. They contrived to possess themselves, with great method and perseverance, of all the avenues to literary fame. Many of them indeed stood high in the ranks of literature and science. The world had done them justice; and in favour of general talents forgave the evil tendency of their peculiar principles. This was true liberality; which they returned by endeavouring to confine the reputation of sense, learning, and taste to themselves or their followers. I will venture to say that this narrow, exclusive spirit has not been less prejudicial to literature and to taste, than to morals and true philosophy. These Atheistical fathers have a bigotry of their own; and they have learnt to talk against monks with the spirit of a monk. But in some things they are men of the world. The resources of intrigue are called in to supply the defects of argument and wit. To this system of literary monopoly was joined an unremitting industry to blacken and discredit in every way, and by every means, all those who did not hold to their faction. To those who have observed the spirit of their conduct, it has long been clear that nothing was wanted but the power of carrying the intolerance of the tongue and of the pen into a persecution which would strike at property, liberty, and life.

~Edmund Burke [1]

---

1. Edmund Burke, "Reflections on the Revolution in France," (1790) in *Works of the Right Honourable Edmund Burke* ,vol. III (of 12), London: John C. Nimmo, 1887, p. 379 (footnote omitted).

3

C CONSERVATIVE ATTITUDE

Writing in the *American Political Science Review* in 1957, Samuel Huntington defined conservatism as that system of ideas employed to defend established institutions when they come under fundamental attack. As Huntington himself put it: "When the foundations of society are threatened, the conservative ideology reminds men of the necessity of some institutions and the desirability of the existing ones."[1] As we have already seen (pp. 2-3) both Michael Oakeshott and Russell Kirk had a completely different opinion about what conservatism is and is not—it is not an ideology, nor a creed, nor a doctrine; it is a "disposition," a "state of mind, a way of looking at the civil social order." And they were absolutely right. Ideology, Russell Kirk argued, makes political compromise impossible. Unlike conservatives, who think of political policies as "intended to preserve order, justice, and freedom," ideologues think of politics "as a revolutionary instrument for transforming society and even transforming human nature;" They vie with one another in paying tribute to their Absolute Truth, without accepting any deviation from it and showing themselves quick to denounce deviationists or defectors from their ideological orthodoxy.[2] And here is how Oakeshott argues on this subject:[3]

> The general characteristics of this disposition are not difficult to discern, although they have often been mistaken. They centre upon a propensity to use and to enjoy what is available rather than to wish for or to look for something else; to delight in what is present rather than what was or what may be. [...]
>
> In short, it is a disposition appropriate to a man who is acutely aware of having something to lose which he has learned to care for; a man in some degree rich in opportunities for enjoyment, but not so rich that he can afford to be indifferent to loss. It will appear more naturally in the old than in the young, not because the old are more sensitive to loss but because they are apt to be more fully aware of the resources of their world and therefore less likely to find them inadequate. In some people this disposition is weak merely because they are ignorant of what their world has to offer them: the present appears to them only as a reside of inopportunities.
>
> To be conservative, then, is to prefer the familiar to the unknown, to prefer the tried to the untried, fact to mystery, the actual to the possible, the limited to the unbounded, the near to the distant, the sufficient to the superabundant, the convenient to the perfect, present laughter to utopian bliss. Familiar relationships and loyalties will be preferred to the allure of more profitable attachments; to acquire and to enlarge will be less important than to keep, to cultivate and to enjoy; the grief of loss will be more acute than the excitement of novelty or promise. It is to be equal to one's own fortune, to live at the level of one's own means, to be content with the want of greater perfection which belongs alike to oneself and one's circumstances. [...]
>
> Moreover, to be conservative is not merely to be averse from change (which may be an idiosyncrasy); it is also a manner of accommodating ourselves to changes, an activity imposed upon all men.

To conclude, here is another excerpt, this time from a famous speech by Abraham Lincoln,[4] in which he explicitly defined ending slavery as a conservative act. This is a great example of true, concrete, non-ideological conservatism.

But you say you are conservative—eminently conservative—while we are revolutionary, destructive, or something of the sort. What is conservatism? Is it not adherence to the old and tried, against the new and untried? We stick to, contend for, the identical old policy on the point in controversy which was adopted by "our fathers who framed the Government under which we live;" while you with one accord reject, and scout, and spit upon that old policy, and insist upon substituting something new. True, you disagree among yourselves as to what that substitute shall be. You are divided on new propositions and plans, but you are unanimous in rejecting and denouncing the old policy of the fathers. Some of you are for reviving the foreign slave trade; some for a Congressional Slave-Code for the Territories; some for Congress forbidding the Territories to prohibit Slavery within their limits; some for maintaining Slavery in the Territories through the judiciary; some for the "gur-reat pur-rinciple" that "if one man would enslave another, no third man should object," fantastically called "Popular Sovereignty;" but never a man among you is in favor of federal prohibition of slavery in federal territories, according to the practice of "our fathers who framed the Government under which we live." Not one of all your various plans can show a precedent or an advocate in the century within which our Government originated. Consider, then, whether your claim of conservatism for yourselves, and your charge or destructiveness against us, are based on the most clear and stable foundations.

The speech, wrote William Henry Herndon, Abraham Lincoln's law partner in Springfield, and later his biographer, "was devoid of all rhetorical imagery, with a marked suppression of the pyrotechnics of stump oratory. It was constructed with a view to accuracy of statement, simplicity of language, and unity of thought. In some respects like a lawyer's brief, it was logical, temperate in tone, powerful—irresistibly driving conviction home to men's reasons and their souls."[5]

1 Samuel Huntington, "Conservatism as an Ideology," *American Political Science Review*, vol. 51, 1957, pp. 454-73 .
2 See Russell Kirk, "The Errors of Ideology" in his *The Politics of Prudence*.
3 Oakeshott, "On Being Conservative" in *Rationalism in Politics*, p.168.
4 Abraham Lincoln, "Cooper Union Address," in Harold Holzer, *Lincoln at Cooper Union: The Speech That Made Abraham Lincoln President*, New York, NY: Simon & Schuster, 2004, p.269
5 William Henry Herndon, Jesse William Weik, Herndon's Lincoln: A True Story of a Great Life – The History and Personal Recollections of Abraham Lincoln, New York, NY: Cosimo, Inc., 2009, p. 455 (originally published 1889).

4

D DECONSTRUCTION

This is not a book for political philosophers, although to some extent it could be regarded as a book on political philosophy for beginners and amateurs of political science. This chapter will therefore focus on a philosophical issue— though not a very "technical" one, nor a very difficult one. To get an idea of what the topic is about, here is an excerpt from G. K. Chesterton:[1]

> Truths turn into dogmas the instant that they are disputed. Thus every man who utters a doubt defines a religion. And the scepticism of our time does not really destroy the beliefs, rather it creates them; gives them their limits and their plain and defiant shape.
>
> We who are Liberals once held Liberalism lightly as a truism. Now it has been disputed, and we hold it fiercely as a faith. We who believe in patriotism once thought patriotism to be reasonable, and thought little more about it. Now we know it to be unreasonable, and know it to be right. We who are Christians never knew the great philosophic common sense which inheres in that mystery until the anti-Christian writers pointed it out to us.
>
> The great march of mental destruction will go on. Everything

will be denied. Everything will become a creed. It is a reasonable position to deny the stones in the street; it will be a religious dogma to assert them. It is a rational thesis that we are all in a dream; it will be a mystical sanity to say that we are all awake.

Fires will be kindled to testify that two and two make four. Swords will be drawn to prove that leaves are green in summer. We shall be left defending, not only the incredible virtues and sanities of human life, but something more incredible still, this huge impossible universe which stares us in the face. We shall fight for visible prodigies as if they were invisible. We shall look on the impossible grass and the skies with a strange courage. We shall be of those who have seen and yet have believed.

~*G. K. Chesterton*

And now let's give the floor to English philosopher Roger Scruton:

The Enlightenment made explicit what had long been implicit in the intellectual life of Europe: the belief that rational inquiry leads to objective truth. Even those Enlightenment thinkers who distrusted reason, like Hume, and those who tried to circumscribe its powers, like Kant, never relinquished their confidence in rational argument. Hume opposed the idea of a rational morality; but he justified the distinction between right and wrong in terms of a natural science of the emotions, taking for granted that we could discover the truth about human nature and build on that firm foundation. Kant may have dismissed "pure reason" as a tissue of illusions, but he elevated practical reason in the place of it, arguing for the absolute validity of the moral law. For the ensuing 200 years, reason retained its position as the arbiter of truth and the foundation of objective knowledge.

Reason is now on the retreat, both as an ideal and as a reality. In place of it has come the "view from outside"—which puts our entire tradition of learning in question. The appeal to reason, we are told, is merely an appeal to Western culture, which has made reason into its shibboleth and laid claim to an objectivity that no culture could possess. Moreover, by claiming reason as its foundation, Western culture has concealed its pernicious ethnocentrism; it has dressed up Western ways of thinking as though they had universal force. Reason, therefore, is a lie, and by exposing the lie we reveal the oppression at the heart of Western culture. Behind the attack on reason lurks another and more virulent hostility: the hostility to the culture and the curriculum that we have inherited from the Enlightenment.[2]

Yes, *reason is now on the retreat*, and if we examine the gurus, the *maîtres à penser* of our times, "those whose works are most often cited in the endless stream of articles devoted to debunking Western culture," we see that they are all bitter enemies and fierce opponents of what once was called objective truth. Their names are Friedrich Nietzsche ("There are no truths, only interpretations"), Michel Foucault, Jacques Derrida, and Richard Rorty. Truth, says Foucault, is not an absolute, "truth is the child of 'discourse,'and as discourse changes, so does the truth contained in it." Truth is the product of an epoch, existing by virtue of the prevailing social "power;" it is what Marx called *ideology*: a collection of ideas with no authority in themselves "but that disguise and mystify the social reality."

Popular for the same reason as Foucault's power analysis, continues Scruton, is the theory of *deconstruction* put forward by Jacques Derrida:

> Nobody knows—or at least nobody has explained—what deconstruction is. But its very obscurity constitutes a large part of its appeal. By offering reams of gobbledygook, the deconstructionist is able to fortify his all-important assumption: that meaning is impossible. There is no such thing as the objective, decidable meaning of a word or argument. In the official jargon, there is no "transcendental signified." Every word, once uttered, is hostage to interpretation, and the decision to interpret the word one way rather than another is in the last analysis political—the only real questions are the old ones uttered by Lenin: Who? and Whom? Who is doing the interpreting, and against whom as his victim? If Dead White Males have

monopolized the interpretation of Jane Austen, for example, is it surprising that the "official" readings of Austen's novels give no real place to women and their aspirations? Is it surprising that these novels are construed as vindications, rather than repudiations, of bourgeois marriage? Confronted by a text from the traditional canon, we can proceed to deconstruct it as we will, for the only constraints that bind us are those that we ourselves have chosen. Deconstructive criticism is like modern productions of traditional theater: the text is read against itself, so as to mean anything that the critic or producer should choose. And invariably the purpose is political: to debunk the old authorities, in the name of liberation.[3]

To return to Chesterton, it's likely that the word "deconstruction" was not in his vocabulary. It's also likely that that term may be more trendy in today's world, but "destruction" has more or less (if not exactly) the same meaning.

How to fight against this "culture of repudiation?" In his books Scruton offers penetrating attacks on deconstruction, on Foucault, on Nietzsche, etc. His main argument is very straightforward, therefore absolutely conservative:

A writer who says that there are no truths, or that all truth is "merely relative," is asking you not to believe him. So don't. Deconstruction deconstructs itself, and disappears up its own behind, leaving only a disembodied smile and a faint smell of sulphur.[4]

1   G. K. Chesterton, *Heretics*, New York: John Lane Company, 1905, pp. 304-305.
2   Roger Scruton, "What Ever Happened to Reason?" *City Journal*, Spring 1999.
3   *Ibid.*
4   Roger Scruton, *Modern Philosophy*, London: Sinclair-Stevenson, 1994, pp. 478-479

5

E EDUCATION

Education is one of the most important issues facing the globalized world in the twenty-first century. In America and the Western world, true conservatives want Education to improve for all future generations, but they know that this is not about public funding, but rather about changing goals, objectives, and methods. Here are a couple of good examples of how this issue can be addressed from a conservative point of view.

> There is need of a sound body, and even more of a sound mind. But above mind and above body stands character—the sum of those qualities which we mean when we speak of a man's force and courage, of his good faith and sense of honor. I believe in exercise for the body, always provided that we keep in mind that physical development is a means and not an end. I believe, of course, in giving to all the people a good education. But the education must contain much besides book-learning in order to be really good. We must ever remember that no keenness and subtleness of intellect, no polish, no cleverness, in any way make up for the lack of the great solid qualities. Self restraint, self mastery, common sense, the power of accepting individual

responsibility and yet of acting in conjunction with others, courage and resolution—these are the qualities which mark a masterful people. Without them no people can control itself, or save itself from being controlled from the outside. I speak to brilliant assemblage; I speak in a great university which represents the flower of the highest intellectual development; I pay all homage to intellect and to elaborate and specialized training of the intellect; and yet I know I shall have the assent of all of you present when I add that more important still are the commonplace, every-day qualities and virtues.

~Theodore Roosevelt [1]

In the main, the trouble with American education is that we have put into practice the educational philosophy expounded by John Dewey and his disciples. In varying degrees we have adopted what has been called "progressive education."

Subscribing to the egalitarian notion that every child must have the same education, we have neglected to provide an educational system which will tax the talents and stir the ambitions of our best students and which will thus insure us the kind of leaders we will need in the future.

In our desire to make sure that our children learn to "adjust" to their environment, we have given them insufficient opportunity to acquire the knowledge that will enable them to master their environment.

In our attempt to make education "fun," we have neglected the academic disciplines that develop sound minds and are conducive to sound characters.

Responding to the Deweyite attack on methods of teaching, we have encouraged the teaching profession to be more concerned with how a subject is taught than with what is taught. Most important of all: in our anxiety to "improve" the world and insure "progress" we have permitted our schools to become laboratories for social and economic change according to the predilections of the professional educators. We have forgotten that the proper function of the school is to transmit the cultural heritage of one generation to the next generation, and to so train the minds of the new generation as to make them capable of absorbing ancient learning and applying it to the problem of its own day.

The fundamental explanation of this distortion of values is that we have forgotten that purpose of education. Or better: we have forgotten for whom education is intended. The function of our schools is not to educate, or elevate, society; but rather to educate individuals and to equip them with the knowledge that will enable them to take care of society's needs. We have forgotten that a society progresses only to the extent that it produces leaders that are capable of guiding and inspiring progress. And we cannot develop such leaders unless our standards of education are geared to excellence instead of mediocrity. We must give full rein to individual talents, and we must encourage our schools to enforce the academic disciplines—to put preponderant emphasis on English, mathematics, history, literature, foreign languages and the natural sciences. We should look upon our schools—not as a place to train the "whole character" of the child—a responsibility that properly belongs to his family and church—but to train his mind.

Our country's past progress has been the result, not of the mass mind applying average intelligence to the problems of the day, but of the brilliance and dedication of wise individuals who applied their wisdom to advance the freedom and the material well-being of all of our people. And so if we would improve education in America—and advance the fortunes of freedom—we will not rush to the federal treasury with requests for money. We will focus attention on our local community, and make sure that our schools, private and public, are performing the job the Nation has the right to expect of them.

~Barry Goldwater [2]

Another example of a conservative approach to this issue is given by the following excerpt from an article by English philosopher Roger Scruton.[3] He explains what he and his wife Sophie think about the British educational system, and talks about their worries with regard to their son's education.

What passes for education in many British schools is really a process of demoralization, in which children are taken from their parents and surrendered to their peers. Today, significant numbers of young Britons leave school unable to read or do mental arithmetic. [...] As for manners, these have declined to such an extent that shops near London schools regularly close their doors to children, while older people seek refuge in another car when children board a train.

Instead of preparing children for adult life, our system of education ensures that they remain children, with all of childhood's self-centered incompetence but none of its redeeming innocence and shame. The state's attempt to sexualize children—encouraging members of the younger generation to master all the relevant positions by the age of 14, and making homosexuality a central part of their curriculum—doesn't help matters. Sex, pupils learn, is just an extension of childhood—another realm of play, in which all is permitted that could lead to enjoyment, and in which only the serious, the lasting, and the loving are dangerous. [...]

The new curriculum, which has both the aim and the effect of cutting off children from their parents, making them unlovable to adults and the exclusive property of the state, springs from the minds of people who are themselves, for the most part, childless. It would be better, it seemed to us, for Sam to be sent down a coal mine, there to encounter the real world of adults, than to go through the complete course in demoralization that our rulers require. Even the private schools must follow the National Curriculum, which has been carefully devised to remove all the knowledge that Sophie and I value and to substitute the "life skills" needed in an urban slum.

The only solution that has occurred to us so far is to educate Sam ourselves for as long as time, energy, and knowledge permit

[...]. As to what Sam's curriculum should be, common sense directs us down the old and beaten path. And we shall start him off with Grimm, Andersen, and Lewis Carroll, since their brand of children's literature does not merely enlarge the imagination: it also educates the moral sense.

While pondering this matter, however, I was invited by a national newspaper to describe what we intended for Sam—a sign that many people share our concerns. [...]

The article precipitated a storm of abuse from experts in child-rearing, educational gurus, feminists, and assorted believers in progress—all manifestly products of an education system that identifies irony as an elitist crime and has therefore extinguished the ability to understand it. For several weeks, we lived in dread of the social workers. If we could not answer their inquiries, we feared, Sam would be put into foster care, denied all access to his parents, and given a normal diet of pop, television, and takeout.

1   Theodore Roosevelt, "Citizenship in a Republic," an address delivered at the Sorbonne, in Paris, France, April 23, 1910. Originally published 1910: Theodore Roosevelt, *African and European Addresses*, with an introduction presenting a description of the conditions under which the addresses were given during Mr. Roosevelt's journey in 1910 from Khartoum through Europe to New York, by Lawrence F. Abbott. III. N.Y.: G.P. Putnam's Sons. 1910 (now available for free download at Project Gutenberg: www.gutenberg.org).

2   Barry Goldwater, *The Conscience of a Conservative*, Washington, D.C.: Regnery Gateway, Inc., 1990, pp.77-79.

3   Roger Scruton, "Becoming a Family," *City Journal*, Spring 2001.

6

F FAMILY VALUES

There is not conservatism; there are conservatisms. There are neocons and paleocons, theocons and crunchy cons, social conservatives and fiscal conservatives[1]... That's why perhaps the best way to understand what we are talking about when we refer to someone as a conservative is by asking the question, "What do you want to conserve?" Russell Kirk once answered,[2] "The institution most essential to conserve is the family." Which, of course, makes him a social conservative, or if you prefer a "Burkean conservative" (whose basic political principles are based on the ancient classical and Christian moral natural law, derived from God and perceived by all uncorrupted men through "right reason"):

> Men and nations are governed by moral laws; and those laws have their origin in a wisdom that is more than human—in divine justice. At heart, political problems are moral and religious problems. The wise statesman tries to apprehend the moral law and govern his conduct accordingly. We have a moral debt to our ancestors, who bestowed upon us our civilization, and a moral

obligation to the generations who will come after us. This debt is ordained of God. We have no right, therefore, to tamper impudently with human nature or with the delicate fabric of our civil social order.[3]

In the same line of thought Roger Scruton argues that two basic views exist of society and politics: *contractual*, which is the liberal view, and *family* (or transcendent) which is the conservative view. Like Robert Filmer in the 17th century, he thinks that conceiving or imagining political society as a contract between people is unrealistic, and that the family is by far a better model for understanding political society.

Of course, it goes without saying that, in this perspective, protecting and preserving the family and its values as an institution is protecting society and promoting the common good. But what are those family values? First and foremost, let's say that, at least since the time of the Roman empire, they are inextricably entwined with religious beliefs—the early Christians "chose the domain of family values to mark themselves off from their non-Christian neighbors," and "the early Church fathers preached against divorce, against infanticide and abortion, and against sexual activity outside marriage."[4] Today in the U.S., for instance, social conservatives use the term "family values" to support traditional morality and Christian values. Therefore they oppose legalized induced abortion, pornography, pre-marital sex, cohabitation, polygamy, homosexuality and same-sex marriage, certain aspects of feminism, etc. At the same time they support abstinence education and policies aimed to protect children from obscenity and exploitation.

Yet, sometimes things don't work out the way one might have anticipated: on February 6, 2013, in the U.K. more than half of the Tory party failed to support Conservative

Prime Minister David Cameron on his opposition to gay marriage, an issue he had personally invested in—but Conservatives know that human nature is not and never will be perfect... Be it as it may, here is what Roger Scruton had to say about that:[5]

> Our situation today mirrors that faced by Burke. Now, as then, abstract ideas and utopian schemes threaten to displace practical wisdom from the political process. Instead of the common law of England we have the abstract idea of human rights, slapped upon us by European courts whose judges care nothing for our unique social fabric. Instead of our inherited freedoms we have laws forbidding "hate speech" and discrimination that can be used to control what we say and what we do in ever more intrusive ways.
>
> The primary institutions of civil society—marriage and the family—have no clear endorsement from our new political class. Most importantly, our parliament has, without consulting the people, handed over sovereignty to Europe, thereby losing control of our borders and our collective assets, the welfare state included. [...]
> Conservatives believe, with Burke, that the family is the core institution whereby societies reproduce themselves and pass moral knowledge to the young. The party has made a few passing nods in this direction, but its only coherent policy—sprung on the electorate without forewarning—is the introduction of gay marriage. Sure, there are arguments for and against this move. But for the ordinary voter the family is a place in which children are produced, socialised and protected. That is what the party should be saying, but does not say, since it is prepared to sacrifice the loyalty of its core constituents to the demands of a lobby that is unlikely to vote for it.

1   See Appendix 1 of this book ("Kinds of Conservatism").
2   Russell Kirk, "May the Rising Generation Redeem the Time?" in his *The Politics of Prudence*, Wilmington, DE: ISI Books, 1993 (originally a lecture given at the Heritage Foundation, December 11, 1991), p. 301.

3   Russell Kirk, *The Intelligent Woman's Guide to Conservatism*, New York: The Devin-Adair Company, 1957, p. 14.
4   Richard P. Saller, "Family Values in Ancient Rome," Fathom Archive (University of Chicago Library - Digital Collections), Copyright 2001 The University of Chicago, http://fathom.lib.uchicago.edu/1/777777121908/.
5   Roger Scruton, "Identity, family, marriage: our core conservative values have been betrayed," *The Guardian* ("Comment is free"), Saturday 11 May 2013, http://www.theguardian.com/commentisfree/2013/may/11/identity-family-marriage-conservative-values-betrayed

7

G GUNS

"I have a very strict gun control policy: if there's a gun around, I want to be in control of it." Thus spoke Clint Eastwood, and his saying, humor included, is perhaps representative of the attitude most conservative Americans have regarding this issue. On the other hand, as Tim Stanley, a British historian of the United States, pointed out in his *Telegraph* blog,[1]

> Gun ownership isn't just constitutionally protected—it actually reflects the spirit of the American Revolution. The Founding Fathers were terrified of tyranny reasserting itself, so when they created a democracy they framed it as a constitutional republic bound by limits. Ergo, the Second Amendment gives individuals and communities the leverage of physical self-defence: they can protect themselves against potential state terror.

A question many advocates of gun control keep asking gun owners is "why do you *need* to own an assault weapon?" To them, writes Stanley, the question is "redundant." If the Constitution says that they can, then they will.

This Don't Tread On Me spirit might strike the liberal as pure bloodymindedness [...], but it's also the product of a culture that prioritises individual liberty over corporate responsibility. Moreover, a conservative would argue that an assault weapon is only an assault weapon if used to *assault* someone—and in a healthier society that would happen as rarely as possible. [...] America is awash with guns to the point where they have become part of the fabric of the social order. That means that while they are the source of anarchy, they can also be interpreted as something that keeps the peace. Conservatives argue that because criminals have ready access to guns then it's only fair to even the odds for potential victims by permitting them to own them, too.[2]

But if, as Stanley puts it, gun ownership reflects the spirit of the American Revolution, it was Cesare Beccaria—an 18th-century Italian philosopher whose work had a considerable influence on the development of U.S. law—who, perhaps more than any other thinker, offered a valid contribution to the pro-gun ownership cause. He maintained that "if guns are outlawed, only outlaws will have guns," a logical argument in his masterpiece *On Crimes and Punishments* (1764), published a full quarter-century before the Second Amendment was proposed:

False is the idea of utility that sacrifices a thousand real advantages for one imaginary or trifling inconvenience; that would take fire from men because it burns, and water because one may drown in it; that has no remedy for evils except destruction. The laws that forbid the carrying of arms are laws of such a nature. They disarm only those who are neither inclined nor determined to commit crimes.

Can it be supposed that those who have the courage to violate the most sacred laws of humanity, the most important of the code, will respect the less important and arbitrary ones, which can be violated with ease and impunity, and which, if strictly obeyed, would put an end to personal liberty... and subject innocent persons to all the vexations that the guilty alone ought to suffer?

Such laws make things worse for the assaulted and better for the assailants; they serve rather to encourage than to prevent homicides, for an unarmed man may be attacked with greater confidence than an armed man. They ought to be designated as laws not preventive but fearful of crimes, produced by the tumultuous impression of a few isolated facts, and not by thoughtful consideration of the inconveniences and advantages of a universal decree.[3]

To conclude, let's quote a Founding Father whose conservatism has been often, yet wrongly, questioned:[4]

A strong body makes the mind strong. As to the species of exercise, I advise the gun. While this gives a moderate exercise to the body, it gives boldness, enterprise, and independence to the mind. Games played with the ball, and others of that nature, are too violent for the body, and stamp no character on the mind. Let your gun therefore be the constant companion of your walks.

1   Tim Stanley, "For the attention of Piers Morgan: three reasons why conservatives oppose gun control," Tim Stanley's blog at *The Telegraph*, January 17, 2013: http://blogs.telegraph.co.uk/news/timstanley/100198584/for-the-attention-of-piers-morgan-three-reasons-why-conservatives-oppose-gun-control/
2   *Ibid.*
3   Cesare Beccaria, *Dei delitti e delle pene*, [*On Crimes and Punishments*] ch.38 (1764) Translation is as quoted by Thomas Jefferson in his *Commonplace Book*, 314 (G. Chinard ed. 1926).
4   Thomas Jefferson, Jefferson to Peter Carr, *The Papers of Thomas Jefferson*,

Princeton: Princeton University Press, 1950-. 33 vols, 8:406-8. A free online version of this edition is now available from the National Archives through the Founders Online Project.

As for whether Jefferson was a Conservative or not, the sixth and last volume of Dumas Malone's *Jefferson and His Time*, *The Sage of Monticello* (Little Brown and Company; 1st edition, July 1981), corrects several generations of distortion. "When viewed in retrospect," he writes, "his reaction to the economic problems of his day can better be described as conservative." Furthermore, "Jefferson championed public education," writes Clyde Wilson ("Thomas Jefferson, Conservative" in *From Union to Empire: Essays in the Jeffersonian Tradition*, The Foundation for American Education, 2003, p.34) but "it was not public education on the leveling Prussian-New England model that later became the American standard. The traditional classical curriculum was to be supplemented by more modern and practical subjects, but not jettisoned to make room for them. It was to be an education competitive, elitist, based on a belief in a natural aristocracy of talents and virtues. The rich would always take care of themselves. The purpose of public education was to make sure that the talented ones who appeared among the poor would not be lost. That is the exact opposite of what modern American public education aims at, for its goal is to reduce the educational level to the lowest common denominator—which, in effect, guarantees that the poor but promising youth does not learn enough to rise above his station or to compete with the privileged."

8

H HISTORY

Institutions which have existed over a long period of time have a reason and purpose inherent in them, a collective wisdom incarnate in them, and the fact that we don't perfectly understand or cannot perfectly explain why they 'work'is no defect in them but merely a limitation in us.

~*Irving Kristol* [1]

People will not look forward to posterity, who never look backward to their ancestors.

~*Edmund Burke* [2]

As we have seen in the first chapter, the U.S. Constitution was seen by the Founding Fathers as an extension of the ideas of the Magna Carta and the English Bill of Rights. Even more so, in Thomas Jefferson's opinion the "new" rights guaranteed by the English Bill of Rights were not new at all. In fact, they were held to be the Germanic liberties—stolen by the Normans during their conquest of

England—of the ancient Anglo-Saxons, as the account of the Germans written by the Roman historian Tacitus shows.

Thomas Jefferson and other early American revolutionaries were immersed in myths of Anglo-Saxon democracy. So indebted did Jefferson feel to Anglo-Saxon culture and what he took to be its legacy of Germanic liberties that he planned to put two Anglo-Saxon heroes, Hengist and Horsa—invited by Vortigern into Britain, according to Bede's *History of the English Church and People*, to aid in the defense of the country against enemies to the north—on the great seal of the new republic, whose obverse side would bear an image of the pillar of fire that led the Chosen People into the Promised Land (Exodus 13:21-22). According to John Adams, to whom he had communicated his wishes, Jefferson saw Hengist and Horsa as representing "the form of government we have assumed," thereby tracing American democratic institutions to their origins in the social practices of the pre-Christian Germanic peoples.[3]

In other words, the Founding Fathers were history-oriented and, *therefore*, conservative in the truest sense of the word. That's why Edmund Burke liked the American Revolution as much as he disliked the French Revolution.

Yet, as Burke[3] himself put it, "We do not draw the moral lessons we might from history." On the contrary,

without care it may be used to vitiate our minds and to destroy our happiness. In history a great volume is unrolled for our instruction, drawing the materials of future wisdom from the past errors and infirmities of mankind. It may, in the perversion, serve for a magazine furnishing offensive and defensive weapons for parties in church and state, and supplying the means of keeping alive or reviving dissensions and animosities, and adding fuel to civil fury.

History consists for the greater part of the miseries brought upon the world by pride, ambition, avarice, revenge, lust, sedition, hypocrisy, ungoverned zeal, and all the train of disorderly appetites which shake the public with the same

"troublous storms that toss
The private state, and render life unsweet."
(From Edmund Spenser, *The Faerie Queene*, II, canto 7. xiv.)

These vices are the causes of those storms. Religion, morals, laws, prerogatives, privileges, liberties, rights of men, are the *pretexts*. The pretexts are always found in some specious appearance of a real good. You would not secure men from tyranny and sedition, by rooting out of the mind the principles to which these fraudulent pretexts apply? If you did, you would root out every thing that is valuable in the human breast. As these are the pretexts, so the ordinary actors and instruments in great public evils are kings, priests, magistrates, senates, parliaments, national assemblies, judges, and captains. You would not cure the evil by resolving, that there should be no more monarchs, nor ministers of state, nor of the gospel; no interpreters of law; no general officers; no public councils. You might change the names. The things in some shape must remain. A certain *quantum* of power must always exist in the community, in some hands, and under some appellation.

Wise men will apply their remedies to vices, not to names; to the causes of evil which are permanent, not to the occasional organs by which they act, and the transitory modes in which they appear. Otherwise you will be wise historically, a fool in practice. Seldom have two ages the same fashion in their pretexts and the same modes of mischief. Wickedness is a little more inventive. Whilst you are discussing fashion, the fashion is gone by. The very same vice assumes a new body. The spirit transmigrates; and, far from losing its principle of life by the change of its appearance, it is renovated in its new organs with the fresh vigour of a juvenile activity. It walks abroad; it continues its ravages; whilst you are gibbeting the carcass, or demolishing the tomb. You are terrifying yourself with ghosts and apparitions, whilst your house is the haunt of robbers.

It is thus with all those, who, attending only to the shell and husk of history, think they are waging war with intolerance, pride, and cruelty, whilst, under colour of abhorring the ill principles of antiquated parties, they are authorizing and feeding the same odious vices in different factions, and perhaps in worse.[4]

1   Irving Kristol, "Utopianism, Ancient and Modern," in his *Two Cheers for Capitalism*, New York: Basic Books, 1978, p. 161.
2   Burke, "Reflections on the Revolution in France," (1790) in *Works of the Right Honourable Edmund Burke* ,vol. III (of 12), pp. 208-209.
3   Gabrielle M. Spiegel, "In the Mirror's Eye: The Writing of Medieval History in America," Anthony Molho and Gordon S. Wood (ed.), *Imagined Histories: American Historians Interpret the Past*, Princeton: Princeton University Press, 1998, p.240.
4   Burke, "Reflections on the Revolution in France," in *Works of the Right Honourable Edmund Burke* ,vol. III (of 12), p. 274.

9

I IDENTITY

"Conservatism is about national identity," writes Roger Scruton.[1] Well, we must admit that the meaning of the term "identity" as we currently use it is not as obvious and self-evident as it might seem, nor is it well defined by dictionaries. Let's say that our present idea of "identity" is a fairly recent social construction, and a rather complicated one at that. Not by chance, within political science we find the concept of "identity" at the center of lively debates in every major field. But this is not the place for such debates, so let's just see what Scruton means when he uses that term. Let's follow his reasoning.[2] We conservatives, he says, believe that our identities and values are formed "through our relations with other people, and not through our relation with the State." In other words, "our rights and responsibilities as individuals are informed by customs that have stood the test of time and have been protected by the rule of law."

Of course, he continues, in the modern world

the State's role is inevitably extensive, but Conservatives believe its reach should always be subject to challenge. It is therefore time to reaffirm the fundamental axiom of conservatism, which is that the State is not an end but a means. Civil society is the end, and the State is the means to protect it.

With that said, Scruton draws up a list of ten principles that "seem to us to be straightforward common sense." At least half of them are closely or somewhat related to the statement with which we began ("Conservatism is about national identity"):

1. The Nation State is the sole vehicle for democratic legitimacy. New Labour sought to weaken the nation externally and divide it internally—externally by its unquestioning acceptance of the primacy of EU supranational authority, internally by indiscriminate immigration and class warfare, which were at the top of the domestic agenda in the time of Blair and Brown. We need to remind the people that as the most elected party in history the Conservatives are dedicated to forging a new unity for our country, one that will integrate all our communities into a shared national idea.

2. Civil society depends upon a common loyalty and a territorial law, and these cannot be achieved or retained without borders. Immigration must therefore be controlled and contained. [...] With its open welfare system, its universal language, its relative wealth and its carefully defended freedoms our country is the preferred destination of Europe's new wave of migrants. Our services and infrastructure are being stretched to breaking point, and our legal and political culture is at risk from communities who cannot or will not endorse it. If we do not take the need for restraint as our starting point we forfeit the right to call ourselves One Nation Conservatives.

3. The nation state requires the sovereignty of Parliament. The right to vote out our rulers and to change our law is the premise of democratic politics. We willingly sacrifice some independence to conduct international trade and to use the world's sea, air and wireless lanes. But whenever possible our law should be made in

Westminster, or in the common-law courts of our kingdom—not by unelected bureaucrats in Brussels nor by courts of European judges. Our taxes too should be fixed by our elected representatives in a sovereign Parliament.

4. As believers in civil society conservatives must protect the institutions and customs that turn human animals into responsible citizens. Ours is a tolerant society, in which liberty is extended to a variety of religions, world-views, and forms of domestic life. But, as Locke argued three centuries ago, liberty is threatened by licence: liberty is founded on personal responsibility and a respect for others, whereas licence is a way of exploiting others for purely personal gain. [...]

5. We must make the environment, the countryside, and the settled communities of our nation into priorities of government. Conservatism is a philosophy of inheritance and stewardship; it does not squander resources but conserves and enhances them. Environmental politics therefore needs to be rescued from the phony expertise of the scare-mongers and from the top-down manipulation of the activists. Properly understood, environmental protection is not a left-wing but a conservative cause.

Another English philosopher, Michael Oakeshott, forty years earlier, had written that

change is a threat to identity, and every change is an emblem of extinction. But a man's identity (or that of a community) is nothing more than an unbroken rehearsal of contingencies, each at the mercy of circumstance and each significant in proportion to its familiarity. It is not a fortress into which we may retire, and the only means we have of defending it (that is, ourselves) against the hostile forces of change is in the open field of our experience; by throwing our weight upon the foot which for the time being is most firmly placed, by cleaving to whatever familiarities are not immediately threatened and thus assimilating what is new without it becoming unrecognizable to ourselves. The Masai, when they were moved from their old country to the present Masai reserve in Kenya, took with them the names of their hills and plains and rivers and gave them to the hills and plains and rivers of the new country. And it is by some such subterfuge of conservatism that every man or people compelled to suffer a notable change avoids the shame of extinction.

As for the United States, the conservative belief in American exceptionalism and the practical identification of American exceptionalism with the American national identity are well known. It was during the 19th century when the French political thinker and historian Alexis de Tocqueville first wrote about this in his most famous work, *Democracy in America*[4] (1835-1840):

> Thus the situation of the Americans is entirely exceptional, and there is reason to believe that no other democratic people will ever enjoy anything like it. Their wholly Puritan origin; their markedly commercial habits; the very country they inhabit, which seems to discourage study of science, literature, and the arts; the proximity of Europe, which allows them not to study these things without lapsing into barbarism; and a thousand more specific causes, of which I have been able to discuss only the most important—all of these things must have concentrated the American mind in a singular way on purely material concerns. Passions, needs, upbringing, and circumstances all seem to have conspired, in fact, to focus the attention of Americans on this earth. Only religion causes them to cast a fleeting and distracted glance heavenward from time to time.
>
> Let us therefore cease to see all democratic nations in the guise of the American people and try at last to see them as they really are.

"In the United States, patriotic sentiment is pervasive," he wrote elsewhere in the same treatise.[5] Americans, he explained,

> care about their country's interest as though they were their own. They glory in the nation's glory. In its successes they see their own work and are exalted by it. They feel for their homeland a feeling analogous to what a man feels for his family, so that a kind of

egoism also contributes to their interest in the state.

In the public official the European often sees nothing but force; the American sees right. Thus one can say that in America man never obeys man; he obeys justice, or the law.

Accordingly, his opinion of himself may be inflated, but it is always salutary. He trusts fearlessly in his own powers, which he believes to be equal to any situation. Suppose a person conceives of an idea for a project that has a direct bearing on the welfare of society. It would never occur to him to call upon the authorities for assistance. Instead, he will publicize his plan, offer to carry it out, enlist other individuals to pool their forces with his own, and struggle with all his might to overcome every obstacle. No doubt his efforts will often prove less successful than if the state had acted in his stead. In the long run, however, the overall result of all these individual enterprises will far outstrip anything the government could do.

Tocqueville was a great believer in the American exceptionalism, and this belief helped him understand it— as the famous maxim of St. Anselm of Canterbury reads, *"credo ut intelligam"* (I believe so that I may understand)! Margaret Thatcher was another believer in the American experiment. She once made a simple, yet profound statement: "Europe was created by history. America was created by philosophy." Theodore Roosevelt was on the same wavelength when he said that "Americanism is a matter of the spirit, and of the soul." He was speaking to the largely Irish Catholic Knights of Columbus at Carnegie Hall on Columbus Day 1915.[6] Another great quote to ponder on, which however strange it may seem is about— the hyphen…

There is no room in this country for hyphenated Americanism. When I refer to hyphenated Americans, I do not refer to naturalized Americans. Some of the very best Americans I have ever known were naturalized Americans, Americans born abroad. But a hyphenated American is not an American at all…

Americanism is a matter of the spirit, and of the soul... The one absolutely certain way of bringing this nation to ruin, of preventing all possibility of its continuing to be a nation at all, would be to permit it to become a tangle of squabbling nationalities, an intricate knot of German-Americans, Irish-Americans, English-Americans, French-Americans, Scandinavian-Americans or Italian-Americans, each preserving its separate nationality, each at heart feeling more sympathy with Europeans of that nationality, than with the other citizens of the American Republic... There is no such thing as a hyphenated American who is a good American. The only man who is a good American is the man who is an American and nothing else.

On January 6, 2011, at the opening of the House of Representatives there was a highly symbolic moment with a reading of the U.S. Constitution. This had never occurred before. Why? Perhaps, as Charles Krauthammer put it in the *Washington Post*, (a great, "pedagogical" piece![7]) for the simple reason that it had never been so needed. And as a matter of fact, after fighting for decades over "who owns the American flag," now the core of the debate between Democrats and Republicans is over "who owns the Constitution." A healthier debate, said Krauthammer, because flags might be regarded as pure symbolism, while the Constitution concretely defines the nature of a country's social contract.

Americans are in the midst of a great national debate over the power, scope and reach of the government established by that document. The debate was sparked by the current administration's bold push for government expansion—a massive fiscal stimulus, Obamacare, financial regulation and various attempts at controlling the energy economy. This engendered a popular reaction, identified with the Tea Party but in reality far more widespread, calling for a more restrictive vision of government

more consistent with the Founders'intent.
Call it constitutionalism.

Constitutionalism. Namely, "the intellectual counterpart and spiritual progeny" of the *originalism* movement in jurisprudence. And, like the latter, the former will require careful and thoughtful development. "But its wide appeal and philosophical depth make it a promising first step to a conservative future."

1   Scruton, "Identity, family, marriage: our core conservative values have been betrayed."
2   Roger Scruton, "What Do Conservatives Believe?" *ConservativeHome* (Britain's leading Conservative blog for news, comment, analysis and campaigns), January 6, 2014, http://www.conservativehome.com/platform/2014/01/roger-scruton-what-do-conservatives-believe.html
3   Oakeshott, "On Being Conservative" in *Rationalism in Politics*, p.168.
4   Alexis de Tocqueville, *Democracy in America*, New York, N.Y.: Library of America, 2004, pp. 517-518.
5   *Ibid.* pp. 106-107.
6   "Roosevelt Bars the Hyphenated," *New York Times*, October 13, 1915
7   Charles Krauthammer, "Constitutionalism," *The Washington Post*, Friday, January 7, 2011. www.washingtonpost.com/wp-dyn/content/article/2011/01/06/AR2011010604379.htm

10

J JUSTICE

My Lords, it has pleased Providence to place us in such a state that we appear every moment to be on the verge of some great mutations. There is one thing, and one thing only, which defies all mutation; that which existed before the world, and will survive the fabric of the world itself,—I mean justice; that justice which, emanating from the Divinity, has a place in the breast of every one of us, given us for our guide in regard to ourselves, and with regard to others, and which will stand, after this globe is burned to ashes, our advocate or our accuser before the great Judge, when He comes to call upon us for the tenor of a well-spent life.

~*Edmund Burke*[1]

Conservatives, says Roger Scruton,[2] believe in respect for individual freedom and for the agreements, customs and institutions that flow from it. "Justice," he explains, "means ensuring that the obligations that arise naturally between free and accountable agents obtain the recognition and protection that they need." Many left-wing ideologues maintain think that people "possess social and economic

rights regardless of how they have conducted their lives."
What is more, he continues,

> [i]ncreasingly these 'human rights' are not confined to negative
> freedoms, such as the rights to life, limb and the pursuit of happiness
> as advocated in the American Declaration of Independence, but
> include positive claims, such as the right to housing, health-care and
> welfare benefits. The ever-expanding grant of these entitlements is
> administered by national and international courts without regard to
> their cost. And the growing injustice, both to honest taxpayers and to
> the future generations who must meet the cost of our present
> extravagance, is justified in the name of 'social justice'. Conservatives
> believe that it is time to move back to a more natural form of justice,
> which rewards responsible behavior and upholds the free agreements
> on which a healthy civil society depends.

Synthetic but effective. Moreover, this is in the same line
of thought as the classical idea of justice. In fact, the
classical definition—coming to us through Plato, Aristotle,
Saint Ambrose, and Saint Augustine of Hippo—is
expressed in a single phrase: *suum cuique*, which means,
translated from Latin, "to each his own." As it is read in
Justinian's Corpus Juris Civilis, "Justice is a habit whereby a
man renders to each one his due with constant and
perpetual will."[3]
Behind the phrase "to each his own," says Russell Kirk,[4]

> lay the beliefs that divine wisdom has conferred upon man a
> distinct nature; that human nature is constant; that the idea of
> justice is implanted in the human consciousness by a transcendent
> power; and that the general rule by which we endeavor to do
> justice is this: "to each man, the things that are his own."
> What is meant by this famous phrase? To put the matter very
> succinctly, the doctrine of *suum cuique* affirms that every man,
> minding his own business, should receive the rewards which are
> appropriate to his work and duties. It takes for granted a society
> of diversity, with various classes and interests. It implies both
> responsibility toward others and personal freedom. It has been a

strong protection for private property, on a small scale or a great; and a reinforcement, for Jews and Christians, of the Tenth Commandment. Through the Roman law, this doctrine of justice passed into the legal codes of the European continent, and even into English and American law. [...]

Edmund Burke re-expressed this doctrine of "to each his own" when, in his Reflections on the Revolution in France, he wrote of true natural rights: "Men have a right to the fruits of their industry, and to the means of making their industry fruitful. They have a right to the acquisitions of their parents, to the nourishment and improvement of their offspring, to instruction in life, and to consolation in death. Whatever each man can separately do, without trespassing upon others, he has a right to do for himself; and he has a right to all which society, with all its combinations of skill and force, can do in his favor."

1   Quoted in Russell Kirk, *Edmund Burke: A Genius Reconsidered,* New Rochelle, N.Y.: Arlington House, 1967, p. 122
2   Scruton, "What Do Conservatives Believe?"
3   Quoted in Russell Kirk, "The Meaning of Justice" (The Heritage lectures), Lecture #457, Heritage Foundation: 1993.
4   *Ibid.*

11

K KIRK (RUSSELL)

Yes, the letter "K" is for Russell Kirk,[1] who is somehow the *genius loci* of this book.

The following excerpt[2]—very enlightening!—is just one out of the many that are worth quoting on this subject. It helps to understand a key aspect of Kirk's work.

In *The Conservative Mind*, Kirk attempted to create a conservative mood rather than an ideological program, and the alternative language he created for conceiving the conservative program remains the most viable in the post-liberal age.

Mystery lay at the heart of Kirk's understanding of the conservative temperament. There is the mystery of free will, of individual choice, of divine Providence, and of the creation and sustaining of tradition. Modernity denigrated mystery in the name of a scientific or politically revolutionary meta-narrative, but "modernity has not discovered convincing answers to the question that these myths raise; rather, modernity has endeavored to shrug away the profound lessons that lie implicit in these myths." The postmodernists, on the other hand, while recognizing mystery, too often use it only as an opportunity for an endless play of meaningless word games. Conservatives, in contrast, keep a healthy respect for the irreducible core of human experience that must be expressed in ways other than through reason: *"Tenebrae are woven into human nature, whatever the meliorists say."* Through his imaginative recreation in *The Conservative Mind* of a tradition that could find a home in a postliberal era, Kirk helped illumine the shadows surrounding the mysteries of life.

1   "For more than forty years, Russell Kirk was in the thick of the intellectual controversies of his time. He is the author of some thirty-two books, hundreds of periodical essays, and many short stories. Both *Time* and *Newsweek* have described him as one of America's leading thinkers, and *The New York Times* acknowledged the scale of his influence when in 1998 it wrote that Kirk's 1953 book *The Conservative Mind* 'gave American conservatives an identity and a genealogy and catalyzed the postwar movement.' Dr. Kirk wrote and spoke on modern culture, political thought and practice, educational theory, literary criticism, ethical questions, and social themes. He addressed audiences on hundreds of American campuses and appeared often on television and radio." Source: *The Russell Kirk Center for Cultural Renewal* (Website: www.kirkcenter.org/index.php)

2   Gerald J. Russello, "Russell Kirk and the Critics" *Intercollegiate Review*, Spring/Summer 2003, 3-13, www.mmisi.org/ir/38_02/russello.pdf. The quotes inside the quote are from: 1) Russell Kirk, "The Salutary Myth of the Otherworldly Journey," The World & I (October 1994): 425-437; 2) Russell Kirk, "A Cautionary Note on the Ghostly Tale" in Watchers at the Strait Gate (Arkham House, 1984), xii.

12

L LAWS

The law is the security of the people of England; it is the security of the people of India; it is the security of every person that is governed, and of every person that governs. There is but one law for all, namely, that law which governs all law, the law of our Creator, the law of humanity, justice, equity,—the Law of Nature and of Nations. So far as any laws fortify this primeval law, and give it more precision, more energy, more effect by their declarations, such laws enter into the sanctuary, and participate in the sacredness of its character. But the man who quotes as precedents the abuses of tyrants and robbers pollutes the very fountain of justice, destroys the foundations of all law, and thereby removes the only safeguard against evil men, whether governors or governed,—the guard which prevents governors from becoming tyrants, and the governed from becoming rebels.

~*Edmund Burke* [1]

Conservatively speaking, there are different theoretical perspectives and approaches to the issue of law. One is exemplified by the above-quoted excerpt from Burke.

Another is cited from Ayn Rand:[2]

There's no way to rule innocent men. The only power any government has is the power to crack down on criminals. Well, when there aren't enough criminals, one *makes* them. One declares so many things to be a crime that it becomes impossible for men to live without breaking laws. Who wants a nation of law-abiding citizens? What's there in that for anyone? But just pass the kind of laws that can neither be observed nor enforced nor objectively interpreted—and you create a nation of law-breakers—and then you cash in on guilt.

And still another, is that of Roger Scruton, which is the most philosophical one. Scruton makes a distinction between abstract and concrete law, asserting that only the latter can truly "fill the vacuum of legitimacy" that presently lies before us. Concrete law, he explains, is exemplified at its best in the English tradition of common law—"law made by judges, in response to the concrete problems that come before them, and in which principles emerge only slowly, and already subject to the harsh discipline of the actual."[3] There are two major threats to concrete law, he continues,

[o]ne is the abolition of judicial independence. This was accomplished by the Communist Party, in the interests of an "abstract" justice—an "equality" of reward—which must inevitably conflict with the concrete circumstances of human existence. The second threat is the proliferation of statute law—of law by decree, law repeatedly made and re-made in response to the half-baked ideas of politicians and their advisors. All such law is fatally flawed: the Communist Party rested its entire claim to legality in the generation of such laws, while removing the only instrument—judicial independence—that could make them into genuine *laws*, rather than military injunctions.

Liberalism has always appreciated the importance of legality. But liberal legality is an abstract legality, concerned with the promotion of a purely philosophical idea of "human rights." What value are human rights, without the judicial process that will uphold them? And besides, in resting one's faith in this beguiling abstraction, does one not also give to one's enemy another bastion against the recognition of his illegitimacy? Is it not possible for him to say that he upholds human rights—only different rights? (The right to work, for instance, or a right to a stake in the means of production.) If one looks back to the French Revolution, one sees just how easy it is for the doctrine of "human rights" to become an instrument of the most appalling tyranny. It suffices to do as the Jacobins did—to abolish the judiciary, and replace it by "people's courts." Then anything can be done to anyone, in the name of the Rights of Man.

In response to liberalism, therefore, it is necessary to work for the restoration of the concrete circumstances of justice. But the concrete law that I have been advocating is very unlike anything that either a socialist or a liberal would approve. It preserves inequalities, it confers privileges, it justifies power. That, however, is also its strength. For there always will be inequalities: there always will be privilege and power. Those are nothing but the lineaments of every actual political order. Since inequalities, privileges, and powers exist, it is right that they should coexist with the law that might justify them. Otherwise they exit unjustified, and also uncontrolled.[4]

1   Edmund Burke, "Speeches in the Impeachment of Warren Hastings, Esquire, Late Governor General of Bengal" (1794), in *Works of the Right Honourable Edmund Burke, Vol. XI.* (of 12), London: John C. Nimmo, 1887, p. 225.
2   Ayn Rand, *Atlas Shrugged*, New York: Plume Reprint Edition, 1999, page 411.
3   Roger Scruton, "How to Be a Non-Liberal, Anti-Socialist Conservative," *The Intercollegiate Review*, 28: 2, Spring 1993, p. 23.
4   *Ibid.*

13

M MAN'S NATURE

Classical liberalism, or liberal individualism, as it is often called, constitutes the core of modern conservatism—not by chance Edmund Burke, widely regarded as the father of modern conservatism, was a Whig rather than a Tory.

Like almost all political ideologies or philosophies, classical liberalism is based on a specific understanding of human nature. The most important point about humans for liberals is the fact that they are individuals. More specifically, within classical liberal discourse, the concept of individual is the nucleus around which the institutions of civil society and government evolve. The well being and prosperity of the individual are the objectives of political organization. As Anthony Arblaster puts it,

> Liberal individualism is both ontological and ethical. It involves seeing the individual as primary, as more 'real' or fundamental than human society and its institutions and structures. It also involves attaching a higher moral value to the individual than to society or to any collective group. In this way of thinking the individual comes before society in every sense.[1]

This conception of human nature somehow implies a high degree of completeness and self-sufficiency on the part of the single human being, which in turn implies that separateness is the fundamental, metaphysical human condition. Therefore, more often than not, the single individual is a radical egoist who enters into interaction with other individuals simply in order to satisfy preconceived preferences. Yet, all things considered, it can be said that classical liberals have an optimistic view of human nature, of man's intelligence, of the possibility of reforming society, and, above all, of the future itself. Liberal thinkers such as John Locke and Jeremy Bentham perceived humans as rational beings who act in their own self-interest by seeking pleasure and avoiding pain. They believed that men could make intelligent and wise choices when given the chance and that these decisions could improve human life and not make it worse. And perhaps here is the greatest difference between classical liberals and conservatives (or at least most of them). In fact, many conservatives adopt an essentially pessimistic view of human nature: in their view human beings may be seen as irrational and untrustworthy, driven not by reason but by basic emotions such as fear, rage excitement, attachment, greed and other emotional preservation impulses. This view may derive in some cases from a religious belief in original sin and in others from more secular beliefs in human frailty. Many conservatives also reject the individualism of classical liberals and follow Thomas Hobbes—the opposite of John Locke in many respects!—in arguing that, were it not for strong institutions, men would be at each others' throats and would constantly view one another with a mix of fear, suspicion and mistrust.

Here is an excerpt from a great political essay by Russell Kirk on conservatism and libertarianism.[2] Published in the fall of 1981, in the earliest days of the Reagan Era, it perfectly illustrates some of the concepts mentioned above.

The ruinous failing of the ideologues who call themselves libertarians is their fanatic attachment to a simple solitary principle—that is, to the notion of personal freedom as the whole end of the civil social order, and indeed of human existence. The libertarians are oldfangled folk, in the sense that they live by certain abstractions of the nineteenth century [...]

What binds society together? The libertarians reply that the cement of society (so far as they will endure any binding at all) is self-interest, closely joined to the nexus of cash payment. But the conservatives declare that society is a community of souls, joining the dead, the living, and those yet unborn; and that it coheres through what Aristotle called friendship and Christians call love of neighbor.

Libertarians (like anarchists and Marxists) generally believe that human nature is good, though damaged by certain social institutions. Conservatives, on the contrary, hold that "in Adam's fall we sinned all": human nature, though compounded of both good and evil, is irremediably flawed; so the perfection of society is impossible, all human beings being imperfect. Thus the libertarian pursues his illusory way to Utopia, and the conservative knows that for the path to Avernus.

The libertarian takes the state for the great oppressor. But the conservative finds that the state is ordained of God. In Burke's phrases, "He who gave us our nature to be perfected by our virtue, willed also the necessary means of its perfection. – He willed therefore the state – He willed its connexion with the source and original archetype of all perfection." Without the state, man's condition is poor, nasty, brutish, and short-as Augustine argued, many centuries before Hobbes. The libertarians confound the state with government. But government—as Burke continued—"is a contrivance of human wisdom to provide for human wants." Among the more important of those human wants is "a sufficient restraint upon their passions. Society requires not only that the passions of individuals should be subjected, but that even in the mass and body, as well as in the individual, the inclinations of men should frequently be thwarted, their will controlled, and their passions brought into subjection. This can be done only by a power out of themselves; and not, in the exercise of its function, subject to that will and to those passions which it is its office to bridle and subdue." In short, a primary function of government is restraint; and that is anathema to libertarians, though an article of faith to conservatives.

However, when we consider human nature it cannot only be in terms of optimism or pessimism. The following excerpt from Barry Goldwater's *The Conscience of a Conservative*[3] illustrates the difference between conservatives and today's liberals:

The root difference between the Conservatives and the Liberals of today is that Conservatives take account of the *whole* man, while the Liberals tend to look only at the material side of man's nature. The Conservative believes that man is, in part, an economic, an animal creature; but that he is also a spiritual creature with spiritual needs and spiritual desires. What is more, these needs and desires reflect the *superior* side of man's nature, and thus take precedence over his economic wants. Conservatism therefore looks upon the enhancement of man's spiritual nature as the primary concern of political philosophy. Liberals, on the other hand,—in the name of a concern for "human beings"—regard the satisfaction of economic wants as the dominant mission of society. They are, moreover, in a hurry. So that their characteristic approach is to harness the society's political and economic forces into a collective effort to *compel* "progress." In this approach, I believe they fight against Nature.

Surely the first obligation of a political thinker is to understand the nature of man. The Conservative does not claim special powers of perception on this point, but he does claim a familiarity with the accumulated wisdom and experience of history, and he is not too proud to learn from the great minds of the past.

The first thing he has learned about man is that each member of the species is a unique creature. Man's most sacred possession is his individual soul—which has an immortal side, but also a mortal one. The mortal side establishes his absolute differentness from every other human being. *Only a philosophy that takes into account the essential differences between men, and, accordingly, makes provision for developing the different potentialities of each man can claim to be in accord with Nature.* We have heard much in the time about "the common man." It is a concept that pays little attention to the history of a nation that grew great through the initiative and ambition of uncommon men. The Conservative knows that to regard man as part of an undifferentiated mass is to consign him to ultimate slavery.

Secondly, the Conservative has learned that the economic and spiritual aspects of man's nature are inextricably intertwined. He cannot be economically free, or even economically efficient, if he is enslaved politically; conversely, man's political freedom is illusory if he is dependent for his economic needs on the State.

The Conservative realizes, thirdly, that man's development, in both its spiritual and material aspects, is not something that can be directed by outside forces. Every man, for his individual good and for the good of his society, is responsible for his *own* development. The choices that govern his life are choices that *he* must make; they cannot be made by any other human being, or by a collectivity of human beings. If the Conservative is less anxious than his Liberal brethren to increase Social Security "benefits," it is because he is more anxious than his Liberal brethren that people be free throughout their lives to spend their earnings when and as they see fit.

1   Anthony Arblaster, *The Rise and Decline of Western Liberalism,* Oxford: Basil Blackwell, 1984, p.15.
2   Burke, "An Appeal from the New to the Old Whigs" (1791) in *Works of the Right Honourable Edmund Burke* ,vol. IV (of 12), p. 176.
3   Goldwater, *The Conscience of a Conservative*, p. 7.

14

N NATURAL ARISTOCRACY

"In all societies," wrote Edmund Burke, "consisting of various descriptions of citizens, some description must be uppermost,"[1] and this uppermost description is the "natural aristocracy," that is "an essential integrant part of any large body rightly constituted." They are the leading, guiding, and governing part of society, "the soul to the body, without which the man does not exist."[2]

But who are the members of this description of citizens? On what basis is this membership established? In Burke's thesis there seems to be some ambiguity here. Perhaps it's not so much ambiguity, but more likely complexity. In fact, he strongly adhered to the traditional system of hereditary privilege. At the same time, he firmly believed that the hereditary aristocracy must be supplemented by persons of exceptional ability from the other classes.

The two following excerpts reveal the complexity of Burke's position.

A true natural aristocracy is not a separate interest in the state, or separable from it. It is an essential integrant part of any large body rightly constituted. It is formed out of a class of legitimate presumptions, which, taken as generalities, must be admitted for actual truths. To be bred in a place of estimation; to see nothing low and sordid from one's infancy; to be taught to respect one's self; to be habituated to the censorial inspection of the public eye; to look early to public opinion; to stand upon such elevated ground as to be enabled to take a large view of the wide-spread and infinitely diversified combinations of men and affairs in a large society; to have leisure to read, to reflect, to converse; to be enabled to draw the court and attention of the wise and learned, wherever they are to be found; to be habituated in armies to command and to obey; to be taught to despise danger in the pursuit of honor and duty; to be formed to the greatest degree of vigilance, foresight, and circumspection, in a state of things in which no fault is committed with impunity and the slightest mistakes draw on the most ruinous consequences; to be led to a guarded and regulated conduct, from a sense that you are considered as an instructor of your fellow-citizens in their highest concerns, and that you act as a reconciler between God and man; to be employed as an administrator of law and justice, and to be thereby amongst the first benefactors to mankind; to be a professor of high science, or of liberal and ingenuous art; to be amongst rich traders, who from their success are presumed to have sharp and vigorous understandings, and to possess the virtues of diligence, order, constancy, and regularity, and to have cultivated an habitual regard to commutative justice: these are the circumstances of men that form what I should call a *natural* aristocracy, without which there is no nation.

The state of civil society which necessarily generates this aristocracy is a state of Nature,—and much more truly so than a savage and incoherent mode of life. For man is by nature reasonable; and he is never perfectly in his natural state, but when he is placed where reason may be best cultivated and most predominates. Art is man's nature. We are as much, at least, in a state of Nature in formed manhood as in immature and helpless infancy. Men, qualified in the manner I have just described, form in Nature, as she operates in the common modification of society, the leading, guiding, and governing part. It is the soul to the body, without which the man does not exist. To give, therefore, no more importance, in the social order, to such descriptions of men than that of so many units is a horrible usurpation.[3]

You do not imagine that I wish to confine power, authority, and distinction to blood and names and titles. No, Sir. There is no qualification for government but virtue and wisdom, actual or presumptive. Wherever they are actually found, they have, in whatever state, condition, profession, or trade, the passport of Heaven to human place and honor. Woe to the country which would madly and impiously reject the service of the talents and virtues, civil, military, or religious, that are given to grace and to serve it; and would condemn to obscurity everything formed to diffuse lustre and glory around a state! Woe to that country, too, that, passing into the opposite extreme, considers a low education, a mean, contracted view of things, a sordid, mercenary occupation, as a preferable title to command! Everything ought to be open,—but not indifferently to every man. No rotation, no appointment by lot, no mode of election operating in the spirit of sortition or rotation, can be generally good in a government conversant in extensive objects; because they have no tendency, direct or indirect, to select the man with a view to the duty, or to accommodate the one to the other. I do not hesitate to say that the road to eminence and power, from obscure condition, ought not to be made too easy, nor a thing too much of course. If rare merit be the rarest of all rare things, it ought to pass through some sort of probation. The temple of honor ought to be seated on an eminence. If it be opened through virtue, let it be remembered, too, that virtue is never tried but by some difficulty and some struggle.[4]

"More than any other order in history, perhaps," wrote Russell Kirk,[5] "the British upper class of the eighteenth and nineteenth centuries deserved this eulogium: as a body, honorable, intelligent, moral, and vigorous."

Like Burke, John Adams, the second president of the

United States, held that every man has equal rights and equal standing before God. At the same time however, men are unequal in their physical and mental capacities, their influence in society, their property and advantages, their piety and iniquity, and almost every other aspect.[6] He also held that a natural aristocracy exercises its authority not solely—nor even primarily—because of wealth nor inherited titles, but because of its possession of virtue and wisdom. This is how he defined the basic characteristics of aristocracy:

> By *natural aristocracy,* in general, may be understood those superiorities of influence in society which grow out of the constitution of human nature. By *artificial aristocracy,* those inequalities of weight and superiorities of influence which are created and established by civil laws. Terms must be defined before we can reason. By aristocracy, I understand all those men who can command, influence, or procure more than an average number of votes; by an aristocracy every man who can and will influence one man to vote besides himself. Few men will deny that there is a natural aristocracy of virtues and talents in every nation and in every party, in every city and village.[7]

Another Founding Father, Thomas Jefferson, who followed John Adams in the White House, had something to say about this. In a letter to Adams[8] he wrote:

> I agree with you that there is a natural aristocracy among men. The grounds of this are virtue and talents. Formerly, bodily powers gave place among the *aristoi* [aristocrats]. But since the invention of gunpowder has armed the weak as well as the strong with missile death, bodily strength, like beauty, good humor, politeness, and other accomplishments, has become but an auxiliary ground for distinction. There is also an artificial aristocracy, founded on wealth and birth, without either virtue or talents; for with these it would belong to the first class. The natural aristocracy I consider as the most precious gift of nature,

for the instruction, the trusts, and government of society. And indeed, it would have been inconsistent in creation to have formed man for the social state, and not to have provided virtue and wisdom enough to manage the concerns of the society. May we not even say, that that form of government is the best, which provides the most effectually for a pure selection of these natural *aristoi* into the offices of government? The artificial aristocracy is a mischievous ingredient in government, and provision should be made to prevent its ascendency.?I think the best remedy is exactly that provided by all our constitutions, to leave to the citizens the free election and separation of the *aristoi* from the *pseudo-aristoi* [pseudoaristocrats], of the wheat from the chaff. In general they will elect the really good and wise. In some instances, wealth may corrupt, and birth blind them, but not in sufficient degree to endanger the society.

It is striking that the philosopher of the common man, the believer in the ordinary man's capacity to govern himself, found himself agreeing with Adams on the crucial importance of the *aristoi*. But perhaps this too is a part of the great American experiment, that is, the creation of a nation based on the principles of freedom, democracy, and meritocracy.

1   Burke, "Reflections on the Revolution in France," p. 295.
2   Russell Kirk, "Libertarians: the Chirping Sectaries" *Intercollegiate Review*, Fall 1981, pp. 345-351, www.mmisi.org/ma/25_04/kirk.pdf.
3   Burke, "An Appeal from the New to the Old Whigs" (1791), pp. 175-176.
4   Burke, "Reflections on the Revolution in France" (1790), p. 297.
5   Kirk, *The Conservative Mind*, p. 63

6   See John Adams, *The Works of John Adams, Second President of the United States: with a Life of the Author, Notes and Illustrations, by his Grandson Charles Francis Adams*, vol. 6 (of 10), Boston: Little, Brown and Co., 1856, p. 454.

7   *Ibid.*, p. 451.

8   Thomas Jefferson to John Adams, Monticello, October 28, 1813, in *Words of the Founding Fathers*, Steve Coffman ed., Jefferson, North Carolina: McFarland & Company, Inc., Publishers, 2012, p. 261.

15

0 ONCE UPON A TIME

Once upon a time we had Ronald Reagan as president.
At that time Americans also had Bob Hope,
Johnny Cash, and Steve Jobs.
Now Barack Obama occupies
the White House
and, oh boy,
what a "change"—we have no jobs,
no cash, and no hope.[1]

Alright, dear readers, I think it's time for me to relax and enjoy some nostalgia. How about you?

I have been told that some Members of Congress disagree with my tax cut proposal. Well, you know it's been said that taxation is the art of plucking the feathers without killing the bird. It's time they realized the bird just doesn't have any feathers left. Maybe some of you heard me put it a different way on several occasions when I've said that robbing Peter to pay Paul won't work anymore, because Peter's been bankrupt for some time now.[2]

∴

I think that you as business men and women know what this regulatory cutback is eventually going to mean to you in savings from paperwork, litigation, and labor. One Ohio businessman wrote to us in this spirit and mentioned his personal frustrations with burdensome regulations. He cited an item from the Toledo area Small Business Association bulletin. Now, actually, when I saw it, I recognized that I had first seen it a number of years ago.

"… It is reported to us" the item said, "that the Lord's Prayer contains 57 words. Lincoln's Gettysburg Address has 266 words. The Ten Commandments are presented in just 297 words, and the Declaration of Independence has only 300 words." And then it goes on to say, "… An Agriculture Department order setting the price of cabbage has 26,911 words." [Laughter]

Well, I thought you'd like to know we've had our researchers working around the clock to find that cabbage regulation. [Laughter] Possibly, the story is more folklore than fact. But whichever, I think it's one case where a bit of folklore can convey a lot of wisdom.

William Freund has said that if the Ten Commandments had been published as government regulations and issued on stone, Moses would have come down from Mt. Sinai with a sprained back and without the tablets. [Laughter][3]

∴

Of course, I can't help but tell you that there are a few signs of advancing years—three particularly. One, you tend to forget things and—I can't remember the other two.[4]

∴

You know economists; economists are the sort of people who see something work in practice and wonder if it would work in theory.[5]

∴

I can't quit without telling you a little story before I sign that— about the recent summit at Williamsburg. I was all set, I couldn't wait for my companions, the leaders of the other several states to come there. And then, when we gathered as we always do, the first meeting is at dinner the night before the conference actually starts. And I was waiting till the first moment of silence as we sat down. And then, I had planned to say to Margaret Thatcher, "Margaret, if one of your predecessors had been a little more clever, you would be hosting this gathering." [Laughter]

But never try to top a lady. As I said, the moment came, and I said, "Margaret, if one of your predecessors had been a little more clever—"She said, "Yes, I know. I would have been hosting this gathering." [Laughter][6]

1   Political joke—with no attribution, as far as I know (and therefore possibly public domain).
2   Ronald Reagan at National League of Cities, Washington, D.C., March 2, 1981, in *The Humor of Ronald Reagan: Quips, Jokes and Anedoctes From the Great Communicator*, Malcolm Kushner ed., Menasha, WI: Museum of Humor.com Press, 2010 (Kindle eBook).
3   Ronald Reagan Remarks at the Annual Washington Policy Meeting of the National Association of Manufacturers, March 18, 1982, www.reagan.utexas.edu/archives/speeches/1982/31882c.htm.
4   Ronald Reagan at Fundraising Brunch in Boca Raton, Florida, September 23, 1988, in *The Humor of Ronald Reagan.*
5   Ronald Reagan, Remarks to Students and Faculty at Purdue University in West Lafayette, Indiana, April 9, 1987, www.reagan.utexas.edu/archives/speeches/1987/040987j.htm.
6   Ronald Reagan, Remarks on Signing the National Tourism Week Proclamation, Washington, D.C., February 1, 1981, www.reagan.utexas.edu/archives/speeches/1984/20184e.htm.

16

P POLITICAL CORRECTNESS

> Political correctness is tyranny with manners.
> ~*Charlton Heston*

"The irony of political correctness," writes Anthony Browne, former director of *Policy Exchange*, the largest center-right think tank in the UK, "is that it is itself almost politically incorrect. Few people like to think of themselves as politically correct, and fewer still would dare publicly admit to it. It is a term generally only used by its detractors."[1] Conservatives are certainly among the greatest detractors of this phenomenon, which is "a heresy of liberalism," as Peter Coleman, an Australian writer and former politician, puts it.[2] "It emerges," he writes, "where liberalism and leftism intersect." "What began as a liberal assault on injustice," he continues, "has come to denote, not for the first time, a new form of injustice."

Concerned about how Political Correctness was trying to overturn the foundations of Western culture and civilization, in 1990 The *New York Times'* culture correspondent Richard Bernstein wrote a landmark thought-provoking article in which he noted that

[c]entral to pc-ness, which has its roots in 1960s radicalism, is the view that Western society has for centuries been dominated by what is often called "the white male power structure" or "Patriarchal hegemony." A related belief is that everybody but white heterosexual males has suffered some form of repression and been denied a cultural voice or been prevented from celebrating what is commonly called "otherness."

"We, the non-Western-Europeans, have no greatness, no culture, no explanations, no beauty, perhaps no humanity," said Amanda Kemp, a student at Stanford University who was active in the campaign three years ago to eliminate a required course in Western civilization. The view that Western civilization is inherently unfair to minorities, women and homosexuals has been at the center of politically correct thinking on campuses ever since the recent debate over university curriculums began.

There is also a school of thought that holds that Political Correctness, or PC, is to culture what Marxism is to economics. First of all, as Bill Lind, former director of the U.S. based Center for Cultural Conservatism, puts it, both Marxism and Political Correctness are totalitarian ideologies (the following excerpt is quite long but well worth it!):

The totalitarian nature of Political Correctness is revealed nowhere more clearly than on college campuses, many of which at this point are small ivy covered North Koreas, where the student or faculty member who dares to cross any of the lines set up by the gender feminist or the homosexual-rights activists, or the local black or Hispanic group, or any of the other sainted "victims" groups that PC revolves around, quickly find themselves in judicial trouble. Within the small legal system of the college, they face formal charges—some star-chamber proceeding—and punishment. [...]

Indeed, all ideologies are totalitarian because the essence of an ideology (I would note that conservatism correctly understood is not an ideology) is to take some philosophy and say on the basis of this philosophy certain things must be true—such as the whole of the history of our culture is the history of the oppression of women. Since reality contradicts that, reality must be forbidden. It must become forbidden to acknowledge the reality of our history. People must be forced to live a lie, and since people are naturally reluctant to live a lie, they naturally use their ears and eyes to look out and say, "Wait a minute. This isn't true. I can see it isn't true," the power of the state must be put behind the demand to live a lie. That is why ideology invariably creates a totalitarian state.

Second, the cultural Marxism of Political Correctness, like economic Marxism, has a single factor explanation of history. Economic Marxism says that all of history is determined by ownership of means of production. Cultural Marxism, or Political Correctness, says that all history is determined by power, by which groups defined in terms of race, sex, etc., have power over which other groups. Nothing else matters. All literature, indeed, is about that. Everything in the past is about that one thing.

Third, just as in classical economic Marxism certain groups, i.e. workers and peasants, are a priori good, and other groups, i.e., the bourgeoisie and capital owners, are evil. In the cultural Marxism of Political Correctness certain groups are good—feminist women, (only feminist women, non-feminist women are deemed not to exist) blacks, Hispanics, homosexuals. These groups are determined to be "victims," and therefore automatically good regardless of what any of them do. Similarly, white males are determined automatically to be evil, thereby becoming the equivalent of the bourgeoisie in economic Marxism.

Fourth, both economic and cultural Marxism rely on expropriation. When the classical Marxists, the communists, took over a country like Russia, they expropriated the bourgeoisie, they took away their property. Similarly, when the cultural Marxists take over a university campus, they expropriate through things like quotas for admissions. When a white student with superior qualifications is denied admittance to a college in favor of a black or Hispanic who isn't as well qualified, the white student is expropriated. [...]

And finally, both have a method of analysis that automatically gives the answers they want. For the classical Marxist, it's Marxist economics. For the cultural Marxist, it's deconstruction. Deconstruction essentially takes any text, removes all meaning from it and re-inserts any meaning desired. So we find, for example, that all of Shakespeare is about the suppression of women, or the Bible is really about race and gender. All of these texts simply become grist for the mill, which proves that "all history is about which groups have power over which other groups." So the parallels are very evident between the classical Marxism that we're familiar with in the old Soviet Union and the cultural Marxism that we see today as Political Correctness.[4]

1 Anthony Browne, *The Retreat of Reason: Political Correctness and the Corruption of Public Debate in Modern Britain*, Lancing, Sussex (U.K.): Harlington Litho Ltd, 2006, p. 1.
2 Peter Coleman, "What Is Political Correctness? The Pros and Cons," *Quadrant Magazine*, Australia. March 2000.
3 Richard Bernstein, "The Rising Hegemony of the Politically Correct," *New York Times*, October 28, 1990.
   www.nytimes.com/1990/10/28/weekinreview/ideas-trends-the-rising-hegemony-of-the-politically-correct.html
4 William S. Lind, "The Origins of Political Correctness," address to 13th Accuracy in Academia conference, George Washington University, July 10, 1998. www.academia.org/the-origins-of-political-correctness/

17

Q QUEST OF THE HOLY GRAIL OF CONSERVATISM

Okay, this is not exactly a chapter, but rather a pause to take stock of the situation with more than half of our "alphabetical journey" behind us.

In practice, there should be enough information to allow readers to answer a question such as, "What is the Holy Grail of conservatism?" Is it the free market or to reduce the federal deficit? Is it the GDP growth or the middle class, or something else? Well, none of these answers—except for "something else," of course—is correct (at least as far as I can tell), nor do I think it's an easy answer…

So, please feel free to try to get the question answered as best as you can.

A little suggestion? Well, here it is:

The conservative is concerned,
first of all,
with the regeneration

*of the spirit and character—with the perennial problem
of the inner order of the soul,
the restoration of the ethical understanding,
and the religious sanction upon which any life worth living is founded.
This is conservatism at its highest.*[1]

1 Kirk, *The Conservative Mind: From Burke to Eliot*, p. 472.

18

R RELIGION

Generally speaking, when we think of conservatism, we think of people with strong religious beliefs. In the same way, when we think of spring we think of the weather getting warmer, flowers beginning to bloom, trees budding and new life starting... And yet, notwithstanding all appearances to the contrary, there is no necessary link between conservatism and religious belief. After all, devout Christians or Jews have embraced a variety of political views and opinions, including liberalism, socialism, and even communism and nationalism, while many of the most important conservative statesmen and thinkers have been agnostics, skeptics, and even atheists. As a matter of fact, as historian Jerry Z. Muller puts it,[1] "despite disagreements as to the *veracity* of religion, conservatives have tended to affirm its *social utility*." Conservatives, he writes,

> make several arguments for the utility of religion: that it legitimates the state; that the hope of future reward offers men solace for the trials of their earthly existence and thus helps to

diffuse current discontent which might disrupt the social order; and that belief in ultimate reward and punishment leads men to act morally by giving them an incentive to do so. Recognition of the social utility of religion is no reflection upon the truth or falsity of religious doctrine. It is quite possible to believe that religion is false but useful. But it is also possible to believe that religion is both useful and true. Or one may believe that religion is "true" in a more rational and universalistic sense than in its particular, historical embodiments, but that those particular embodiments are necessary to make religion accessible to the mass of citizens in a way which is less rationalist and abstract than more intellectual versions of the faith.[2]

From this point of view, the case of the Founding Fathers is emblematic: despite the extreme importance they assigned to religion (and in spite of the fact that most of them were members of Christian churches), only a minority of them accepted orthodox Christian beliefs, attended church regularly, and participated in the sacraments and ordinances. Some were *non-Christian Deists* who rejected all sacraments and rarely attended church, others were *deistic Christians* who attended church regularly or sporadically, but seldom participated in the Lord's Supper and Confirmation.[3] But they definitely agreed that religion was essential in the success of the American experiment. John Adams—who was a Unitarian and a leading example of Christian Deism—put it very clearly:

[W]e have no government armed with power capable of contending with human passions unbridled by morality and religion. Avarice, ambition, revenge, or gallantry, would break the strongest cords of our Constitution as a whale goes through a net. Our Constitution was made only for a moral and religious people. It is wholly inadequate to the government of any other.[4]

And here is an excerpt from George Washington's

"Farewell Address" to the country discussing this very topic:

> Of all the dispositions and habits which lead to political prosperity, religion and morality are indispensable supports. In vain would that man claim the tribute of patriotism who should labor to subvert these great pillars of human happiness, these firmest props of the duties of man and citizens. The mere politician, equally with the pious man, ought to respect and to cherish them. A volume could not trace all their connexions with private and public felicity. Let it simply be asked, Where is the security for property, for reputation, for life, if the sense of religious obligation desert the oaths, which are the instruments of investigation in Courts of Justice?
>
> And let us with caution indulge the supposition that morality can be maintained without religion. Whatever may be conceded to the influence of refined education on minds of peculiar structure, reason and experience both forbid us to expect that national morality can prevail in exclusion of religious principle.[5]

As to Thomas Jefferson's famous "wall of separation between church and state," here is what Russell Kirk had to say:

> Some people persist in fancying that somehow or other the Constitution, or at least the First Amendment, or perhaps the Declaration of Independence, speaks of "a wall of separation" between church and state. But of course no such phrase appears in any American state paper. Those words about the hypothetical "wall," which have provoked so much controversy during the latter half of the 20th-century, occur merely in a letter written in 1802 by Thomas Jefferson, addressed to an assembly of Baptists.[6]

What the Founding Fathers certainly wanted was a nation like the one Alexis de Tocqueville described in *Democracy in America*:

Although religion in the United States never intervenes directly in government, it must be considered as the first of America's political institutions, for even religion does not give Americans their taste for liberty, it does notably facilitate their use of that liberty.

This is how Americans themselves see their religious beliefs. I do not know whether all of them have faith in their religion—for who can read the bottom of men's hearts?—but I am certain that they believe it to be necessary for the preservation of republican institutions.[7]

To conclude (going back to the roots of conservatism), here is an excerpt from Eduard Burke:

We know, and what is better we feel inwardly, that religion is the basis of civil society, and the source of all good and of all comfort. In England we are so convinced of this, that there is no rust of superstition, with which the accumulated absurdity of the human mind might have crusted it over in the course of ages, that ninety-nine in an hundred of the people of England would not prefer to impiety. We shall never be such fools as to call in an enemy to the substance of any system to remove its corruptions, to supply its defects, or to perfect its construction. If our religious tenets should ever want a further elucidation, we shall not call on atheism to explain them. We shall not light up our temple from that unhallowed fire. It will be illuminated with other lights. It will be perfumed with other incense, than the infectious stuff which is imported by the smugglers of adulterated metaphysics. If our ecclesiastical establishment should want a revision, it is not avarice or rapacity, public or private, that we shall employ for the audit, or receipt, or application of its consecrated revenue.—Violently condemning neither the Greek nor the Armenian, nor, since heats are subsided, the Roman system of religion, we prefer the Protestant; not because we think it has less of the Christian religion in it, but because, in our judgment, it has more. We are protestants, not from indifference but from zeal.

We know, and it is our pride to know, that man is by his constitution a religious animal; that atheism is against, not only our reason but our instincts; and that it cannot prevail long. But if, in the moment of riot, and in a drunken delirium from the hot spirit drawn out of the alembick of hell, which in France is now so furiously boiling, we should uncover our nakedness by throwing off the Christian religion which has hitherto been our boast and comfort, and one great source of civilization amongst us, and among many other nations, we are apprehensive (being well aware that the mind will not endure a void) that some uncouth, pernicious, and degrading superstition, might take place of it.[8]

1   Jerry Z. Muller, "Introduction: What Is Conservative Social and Political Thought?" in *Conservatism: An Anthology of Social and Political Thought from David Hume to the Present*, ed. Jerry Z. Muller, Princeton, N. J.: Princeton University Press, 1997, p. 13 [footnotes omitted].

2   *Ibid.*, pp. 13-4.

3   See David L. Holmes, *The Faiths of the Founding Fathers*, New York, N.Y.: Oxford University Press, 2006,

4   John Adams, *The Works of John Adams, Second President of the United States* (Letter to the Officers of the First Brigade of the Third Division of the Militia of Massachusetts, October 11, 1798), Charles Francis Adams, editor, Boston, MA: Little, Brown, and Co. 1854), Vol. IX, p. 229.

5   George Washington, "Address of George Washington, President of the United States and Late Commander-in-Chief of the American Army, to the People of the United States, Preparatory to His Declination," Baltimore: George and Henry S. Keatinge, 1796, pp. 22-23.

6   Russell Kirk, "The First Clause of the First Amendment: Politics and Religion," The Heritage Lectures, # 146, December 9, 1987.

7   Tocqueville, *Democracy in America*, p. 338.

8   Burke, "Reflections on the Revolution in France," pp. 350-351 [footnote omitted].

19

S SOCIAL CONTRACT

The idea of "social contract" needs to be explained through basic questions of political philosophy, such as, "What is the origin of organized society?" or "What is the origin of justice?" The supporters of this idea—that influenced the shapers of the American Revolution and the French Revolution and the constitutions that followed them—make replies that run in terms of *agreement* or *consent* by the individual members of organized society: Organized society came into being as a result of agreements arrived at among its members; it is, therefore, man-made, exactly in the same way as law, justice, and the concepts of right and wrong, are man-made, or artificial.

In spite of their differences, Thomas Hobbes (1588-1679), John Locke (1632-1704), and Jean-Jacques Rousseau (1712-1778)—three key political philosophers—helped develop the social contract theory into what it has become today. They have commonly been linked together also because all three advocate that prior to society men lived in a "state of nature," in which they possessed "natural rights," and that men emerged from the "state of nature" by concluding among themselves a "social contract," by means of which they "surrendered" some, if not all of their "natural rights" to political society.

In particular, Locke made the social contract the basis of his advocacy of popular sovereignty, the idea that the monarch or government must reflect the will of the people. He rejected Hobbes'idea of the "state of nature," believing that society, even prior to the state, is one of freedom and equality of individuals, and that the compact which individuals subsequently conclude with the state has the purpose of securing, not alienating, their "natural rights."

What do conservatives think about the social contract? Well, let's put it this way: conservatives believe in a social contract, albeit a more bare bones version than the one liberals believe in. Edmund Burke, for instance,

> sharply disagreed with the social contract theory of John Locke who saw the state owing its origin to the determination of human beings to enter into a contract agreed upon by them. Burke went deeper, believing that the real contract was with God. As is taught in Romans 13, God created the state; people govern themselves within the context of His will. Burke by no means was a creature of the eighteenth-century Enlightenment.[1]

Now let's cast our attention once more to the father of modern conservatism. The following is perhaps the most celebrated remark in Burke's celebrated *Reflections on the French Revolution*. This passage contains in essence all that he had to say about the social contract throughout most of his *Reflections*. He repudiates the Enlightenment's faith in contract—not merely in the sense of social contract, but in the far more revolutionary sense in which Jean-Jacques Rousseau had used the expression, namely, as the very basic assumption of sovereignty. Burke's definition of social contract derives from his belief that good government is a gift from God. Because government is a divine gift to creation, morality and government cannot be separated. Burke believes that "society is indeed a contract," but unlike Hobbes, Locke, and Rousseau, he believes that it is "a partnership not only between those who are living, but between those who are living, those who are dead, and those who are to be born."

Society is indeed a contract. Subordinate contracts for objects of mere occasional interest may be dissolved at pleasure—but the state ought not to be considered as nothing better than a partnership agreement in a trade of pepper and coffee, calico or tobacco, or some other such low concern, to be taken up for a little temporary interest, and to be dissolved by the fancy of the parties. It is to be looked on with other reverence; because it is not a partnership in things subservient only to the gross animal existence of a temporary and perishable nature. It is a partnership in all science; a partnership in all art; a partnership in every virtue, and in all perfection. As the ends of such a partnership cannot be obtained in many generations, it becomes a partnership not only between those who are living, but between those who are living, those who are dead, and those who are to be born. Each contract of each particular state is but a clause in the great primæval contract of eternal society, linking the lower with the higher natures, connecting the visible and invisible world, according to a fixed compact sanctioned by the inviolable oath which holds all physical and all moral natures, each in their appointed place. This law is not subject to the will of those, who by an obligation above them, and infinitely superior, are bound to submit their will to that law. The municipal corporations of that universal kingdom are not morally at liberty at their pleasure, and on their speculations of a contingent improvement, wholly to separate and tear asunder the bands of their subordinate community, and to dissolve it into an unsocial, uncivil, unconnected chaos of elementary principles. It is the first and supreme necessity only, a necessity that is not chosen, but chooses, a necessity paramount to deliberation, that admits no discussion, and demands no evidence, which alone can justify a resort to anarchy. This necessity is no exception to the rule; because this necessity itself is a part too of that moral and physical disposition of things, to which man must be obedient by consent or force; but if that which is only submission to necessity should be made the object of choice, the law is broken, nature is disobeyed, and the rebellious are outlawed, cast forth, and exiled, from this world of reason, and order, and peace, and virtue, and fruitful penitence, into the antagonist world of madness, discord, vice, confusion, and unavailing sorrow.[2]

1   John M. Pafford, *Russell Kirk*, New York, N. Y.: Bloomsbury, 2013, p. 37.
2   Burke, *Reflections on the French Revolution*, p. 359.

20

T TREE OF LIBERTY

In a letter to Colonel William Smith, John Adams' secretary and future son-in-law, Thomas Jefferson seemed to welcome the so-called Shays' Rebellion—when, in 1786, Farmers in western Massachusetts staged violent protests against new taxes imposed by their state government. "God forbid we should ever be twenty years without such a rebellion," he wrote, "the tree of Liberty must be refreshed from time to time with the blood of patriots & tyrants. It is its natural manure."

Like so many fiscal conservatives and libertarians of our day and age, those farmers "had no love for government, and indeed feared that the natural tendency of government to order and secure the lives of the majority would take away their freedoms."[1]

Here is the full text of Jefferson's famous letter:[2]

TO COLONEL SMITH.
Paris, November 13, 1787.

Sir,

I am now to acknowledge the receipt of your favors of October the 4th, 8th, and 26th. In the last, you apologize for your letters of introduction to Americans coming here. It is so far from needing apology on your part, that it calls for thanks on mine. I endeavor to show civilities to all the Americans who come here, and who will give me opportunities of doing it: and it is a matter of comfort to know, from a good quarter, what they are, and how far I may go in my attentions to them.

Can you send me Woodmason's bills for the two copying presses, for the Marquis de la Fayette and the Marquis de Chastellux? The latter makes one article in a considerable account, of old standing, and which I cannot present for want of this article. I do not know whether it is to yourself or Mr. Adams I am to give my thanks for the copy of the new constitution. I beg leave, through you, to place them where due. It will yet be three weeks before I shall receive them from America. There are very good articles in it; and very bad. I do not know which preponderate. What we have lately read in the history of Holland, in the chapter on the Stadtholder, would have sufficed to set me against a chief magistrate eligible for a long duration, if I had ever been disposed towards one: and what we have always read of the elections of Polish Kings, should have for ever excluded the idea of one continuable for life. Wonderful is the effect of impudent and persevering lying. The British ministry have so long hired their gazetteers to repeat, and model into every form, lies about our being in anarchy, that the world has at length believed them, the English nation has believed them, the ministers themselves have come to believe them, and what is more wonderful, we have believed them ourselves. Yet where does this anarchy exist? Where did it ever exist, except in the single instance of Massachusetts? And can history produce an instance of rebellion so honorably conducted? I say nothing of its motives. They were founded in ignorance, not wickedness. God forbid, we should ever be twenty years without such a rebellion. The people cannot be all, and always, well informed. The part which is wrong will be discontented, in proportion to the importance of the facts they misconceive. If they remain quiet under such misconceptions, it is a lethargy, the forerunner of death to the public liberty. We have had thirteen States independent for eleven years. There has been one rebellion. That comes to one rebellion in a century and a half for each State. What country before ever existed a century and a half without a rebellion? And what country can preserve its liberties, if its rulers are not warned from time to time, that this people preserve the spirit of resistance? Let them take arms. The remedy is to set them right as to facts, pardon, and pacify them. What signify a few lives lost in a century or two? The tree of liberty must be refreshed from time to time with the blood of patriots and tyrants. It is its natural manure. Our convention has been too much impressed by the insurrection of Massachusetts: and on the spur of the moment, they are setting up a kite to keep the hen-yard in order. I hope in God, this article will be rectified before the new constitution is accepted. You ask me, if any thing transpires here on the subject of South America? Not a word. I know that there are combustible materials there, and that they wait the torch only. But this country probably will join the extinguishers. The want of facts worth communicating to you, has occasioned me to give a little loose to dissertation. We must be contented to amuse, when we cannot inform.

Present my respects to Mrs. Smith, and be assured of the sincere esteem of, Dear Sir, your friend and servant,

Th: Jefferson.

1 "Shays's Rebellion (1786)." *Dictionary of American History*. 2003. *Encyclopedia.com*. (May 22, 2014). www.encyclopedia.com/doc/1G2-3401804726.html

2 Thomas Jefferson to Colonel Smith, in *Memoir, Correspondence, and Miscellanies, from the Papers of Thomas Jefferson*, volume II second edition (letter CXIV, November 13, 1787), edited by Thomas Jefferson Randolph, Boston: Gray and Bowen, New York: G. & C. & H. Carvill, 1830. www.gutenberg.org/files/16782/16782-h/16782-h.htm#link2H_4_0116

21

U UTOPIA

As we have already seen in chapter 3, conservatism is not an ideology. On the contrary, conservatives abhor any and all forms of ideology, any and all sets of rigorous political dogmata, in other words, any political religions fanatically advocated and promising the Terrestrial Paradise to the faithful, universal brotherhood and liberation to all, etc.

Edmund Burke was very clear on this. In his biography, *Edmund Burke: A Genius Reconsidered*, Russell Kirk stated:[1]

> But Utopia never will be found here below, Burke knew; politics is the art of the possible, not of perfectibility. We never will be as gods. Improvement is the work of slow exploration and persuasion, never unfixing old interests at once. Mere sweeping innovation is not reform. Once immemorial moral habits are broken by the rash Utopian, once the old checks upon will and appetite are discarded, the inescapable sinfulness of human nature asserts itself: and those who aspired to usurp the throne of God find that they have contrived a terrestrial Hell.

But there are also other ways to look at this issue.

According to Karl Mannheim, for example, Utopia is the will for change; as such, Utopian thought is the major force of historical change.[2] In this light Utopian aspirations are associated with the quest to transcend and/or to transgress existing social roles. Like Weber, Mannheim argues that modern history starts with what he calls "the orgiastic chiliasm of the Anabaptists"—Chiliasm, from the Greek for "one thousand," is originally the early Christian belief that Jesus will return to earth and rule for one thousand years—while modern politics starts when a Utopian mentality (similar to that inspiring the Protestant revolution) brings about the participation of a whole society in the quest for total change. Thus, while ideology reduces the whole social world to a customary procedure, the Utopian thought is always a threat against the routinization of life. In opposition to spiritual chiliasm, there developed an alternative Utopia which Mannheim described as the "conservative Utopian mentality."

So, what does the conservative Utopia look like? Well, first of all let's say that while both liberal and socialist Utopias are future-oriented, the conservative Utopia—perhaps more in the U.K. and the continental Europe than in the U.S.—is oriented towards the past. While both liberal and socialist Utopias depend (most of the time) on legal-rational legitimations, the conservative Utopia depends on traditional ones. Furthermore, it emphasizes not the individual and freedom but nation, authority, and traditional values.[3]

"The meaning of conservatism, as explicated by the Salisbury Group and particularly by Roger Scruton," says Ruth Levitas,[4] "corresponds closely to Mannheim's description." But to be honest it is Scruton himself who thinks that conservatism—"a political practice, the legacy of a long tradition of pragmatic decision making and high-toned contempt for human folly"—is a rejection of utopia for reality, a preference for improving society gradually over fixing society by rubbing it out.[5] Instead of seeking utopian solutions, radical alternatives or bold initiatives, he writes in his 2010 book, *The Uses of Pessimism and the Danger of False Hope,* we should muddle through with "compromise and half measures" mindful that no ultimate solutions are up for grabs.[6]

1   Russell Kirk, *Edmund Burke: A Genius Reconsidered,* Wilmington, DE: Intercollegiate Studies Institute, 2009, p. 166.
2   See Bryan S. Turner, "Introduction," Karl Mannheim, *Ideology and Utopia: Collected Works of Karl Mannheim,* volume 1, New York, N.Y.: Routledge, 1997, xxxiii-lii.
3   See Ruth Levitas, *The Concept of Utopia,* Bern, Switzerland: Peter Lang AG, 2010 (first published in Great Britain in 1990), p. 217.
4   *Ibid.*
5   Raymond Zhong, "Roger Scruton: Want to Save the Planet? Turn Right," *The Wall Street Journal,* April 13, 2012. online.wsj.com/news/articles/SB10001424052702304444604577341521643541262
6   Roger Scruton, *The Uses of Pessimism and the Danger of False Hope,* New York, N.Y.: Oxford University Press, 2010, p. 217

22

V VIRTUE

It is religion and morality alone which can establish the principles upon which freedom can securely stand. The only foundation of a free constitution is pure virtue.

~*John Adams* [1]

In some people I see great liberty indeed; in many, if not in the most, an oppressive, degrading servitude. But what is liberty without wisdom and without virtue? It is the greatest of all possible evils; for it is folly, vice, and madness, without tuition or restraint. Those who know what virtuous liberty is cannot bear to see it disgraced by incapable heads on account of their having high-sounding words in their mouths.

~*Edmund Burke* [2]

It is hardly deniable that the emphasis on virtue (and character) is a conservative characteristic. But here, once again, Conservatism and Americanism are basically indistinguishable. That's also why the content of this chapter is closely related to that of chapter 1. In fact what is presupposed here is Burke's insight into the originally conservative nature of the American Revolution—seen as a conservative movement based on the defense of American rights against the encroachment of the British government intent on exploiting the colonies for economic gain. In other words, to speak of the American Revolution is, in a sense, to speak of conservatism and vice versa.

The American Founding Fathers unanimously agreed that even a perfect plan of government would be not enough to preserve ordered liberty. "Something else was needed," noted historian and political scientist Clinton Rossiter in *The Political Thought of the American Revolution*, "some moral principle diffused among the people to strengthen the urge to peaceful obedience and hold the community on an even keel."[3] Now, as Montesquieu says, as fear is necessary in a despotic government, and honor is mandatory in a monarchy, so virtue is needed in a republic. Which of the above three possibilities did the Americans choose? The answer, of course, was virtue. Here is Rossiter's account of those crucial days:

Revolutionary thinkers drew heavily on their colonial heritage in proclaiming virtue the essence of freedom. The decade of crisis brought new popularity to the cult of virtue that had long held sway in the colonies. All the familiar techniques that earlier colonists had borrowed from England and converted to their purposes were revived for the emergency. The appeal to ancient Rome for republican inspiration was especially favored. The nicest compliment Samuel Adams could pay Joseph Hawley was to say that he had "as much of the stern Virtue and Spirit of a Roman Censor as any Gentleman I ever conversed with." John Dickinson had spoken "with Attick Eloquence and Roman Spirit"; the dead of Concord were "like the Romans of old"; the way to exhort the Americans was to "stir up all that's Roman in them." The Roman example worked both ways: From the decline of the republic Americans could learn the fate of free states that succumb to luxury. [...]The praise of virtue and condemnation of corruption served two very practical purposes in the decade that led to 1776: to mobilize public opinion as sanction for various extra-legal associations and governments, and to tear men loose from their traditional deference to all things British. Most of the ceaseless preaching about "the fatal effects of luxury to a free state" was directed at the mother country. This was especially true in the last months before independence, when men like Edward Bancroft began to argue that the "Effeminacy, Luxury, and Corruption, which extend to all Orders of Men" in England would poison the youthful body of America unless it were to cut short its dependence. [4]

It is also worth noting here that Rossiter sees in the Puritan enterprise the roots of the American idea of virtue and the moral foundations of American democracy and liberty. He writes:[5]

[I]t must never be forgotten, especially in an age of upheaval and disillusionment, that American democracy rests squarely on the assumption of a pious, honest, self-disciplined, moral people.

For all its faults and falterings, for all the distance it has yet to travel, American democracy has been and remains a highly *moral* adventure. Whatever doubts may exist about the sources of this democracy, there can be none about the chief source of the morality that gives it life and substance. From Puritanism, from the way of life that exalted individual responsibility, came those homely rules of everyday conduct—or, if we must, those rationalizations of worldly success—that have molded the American mind into its unique shape. Puritanism was the goad to the American conscience that insisted on communal responsibility before individual freedom, constitutionalism before democracy, order before liberty. If democracy has flourished in these states as strongly as anywhere in the world, it is because we are drawing still upon the moral vigor of Puritanism.

This was the legacy of Puritanism, especially of Congregational Puritanism, to American democracy: the contract and all its corollaries; the higher law as something more than a "brooding omnipresence in the sky"; the concept of the competent and responsible individual; certain key ingredients of economic individualism; the insistence on a citizenry educated to understand its rights and duties; and the middle-class virtues, that high plateau of moral stability on which, so Americans believe, successful democracy must always build. When we recall that the Presbyterian, Baptist, Reformed, and even early Anglican churches in the colonies were likewise Calvinistic, there can be no argument that here was the major religious element in the rise of an American brand of liberty. Early American Protestantism was largely Puritan Protestantism.

Of course, wrote Russell Kirk,[6] Puritanism, and other forms of Calvinism in America,

were Christian in essence, not renewed Judaism merely. And the stern Calvinism of the early colonial years would be modified, presently, by the growth of a less Calvinistic Anglicanism, by the influence of Lutheranism, by the coming of millions of Catholic immigrants in the nineteenth century, and by the arrival of masses of immigrants of other confessions or persuasions. As generation succeeded generation, moreover, the New Englanders themselves would relax the strictness of the founders of Massachusetts Bay Colony.

That said, nevertheless American political theory and institutions, and the American moral order, cannot be well understood, or maintained, or renewed, without repairing to the Law and the Prophets. "In God we trust," the motto of the United States, is a reaffirmation of the Covenants made with Noah and Abraham and Moses and the Children of Israel, down to the last days of prophecy. The earthly Jerusalem never was an immense city: far more Jews live in New York City today than there were inhabitants of all Palestine at the height of Solomon's glory. But the eternal Jerusalem, the city of spirit, still has more to do with American order than has even Boston which the Puritans founded, or New York which the Dutch founded, or Washington which arose out of a political compromise between Jeffersonians and Hamiltonians. Faith and hope may endure when earthly cities are reduced to rubble: that, indeed, is a principal lesson from the experience of Israel under God.

To conclude, the Federalist Papers, which are a series of 85 essays written in 1787 and 1788 to promote the ratification of the United States Constitution, definitely confirm that virtue is a foundation stone of American constitutionalism. "To suppose that any form of government will secure liberty or happiness without any virtue in the people, is a chimerical idea," said James Madison. And Alexander Hamilton said: "The institution of delegated power implies that there is a portion of virtue and honor among mankind which may be a reasonable foundation of confidence."[7]

1   John Adams, *The Works of John Adams, Second President of the United States*, Charles Francis Adams, editor, Boston, Massachusetts: Little, Brown, 1854, Vol. IX, p. 401, to Zabdiel Adams on June 21, 1776.
2   Burke, "Reflections on the Revolution in France," p. 559.
3   Clinton Rossiter, *The Political Thought of the American Revolution*, New York, N.Y.: Harcourt, Brace & World, 1963, p. 199.
4   *Ibid.*, p. 200.
5   Clinton Rossiter, *Seedtime of the Republic: the Origin of the American Tradition of Political Liberty*, New York, N.Y.: Harcourt, Brace, 1953, p. 55.
6   Russell Kirk, *The Roots of American Order*, Wilmington, Delaware: ISI Books, 2003, p. 47.
7   John Jay, James Madison, Alexander Hamilton, *The Federalist Papers*, Saint Louis Park, Minnesota: Filiquarian Publishing, 2007, p. 580.

23

W WELFARE STATE

Needless to say, the Welfare State is a complex phenomenon, maybe too complex to be approached in terms of a single issue. Just to introduce what is going to be the focus of this chapter, let's say that the concept of Welfare State refers to a system of universal social insurance benefits, which are supposed to provide economic safety for the population (and less tangible forms of assistance through the systems of education, health care and social service). One important aspect, among others, of such an enormous and expensive bureaucratic machine is the changes which take place in the social insurance system, its coverage and the generosity of its benefits. This makes any attempt to investigate this issue, or this set of issues, from a political perspective, even more difficult.

However, despite all this, it is not too difficult to identify major differences between the approaches of conservatives and liberals to this complex matter. The following short article[1] by Russell Kirk is a basic example of a conservative approach to the Welfare State:

At the ninth annual forum of Pepperdine College, recently, Mr. Robert Finch, Lieutenant Governor of California, spoke on "The Creative Society of the Future." If we are to be creative, Mr. Finch remarked, we must rise above the old-fangled concept of the welfare state.

Lieutenant Governor Finch speaks with some authority, for last November he received the largest majority ever won by a Republican candidate in California. His campaign was based upon the concept of "the voluntary sector," as contrasted with "the private sector" and "the public sector."

If swelling California, the most populous of states, is marked by a good deal of eccentricity, also it is a state with imagination and vigor. It seems quite possible that California may set the tone for all these United States, in the age which is dawning.

The Civil War, Mr. Finch observed, was fought to preserve the Union against some of the states. Our task a hundred years later, he went on, may be to preserve the Union from the Federal Government.

And the grand difficulties of our age, the Lieutenant Governor said, conspicuously are state and local difficulties: the problems of qualitative improvement hi education, of slums and suburbs, of personal relationships and private rights in a time when consolidation of power and decay of variety menace us all—a time when, in the phrase of Emerson, "things are in the saddle, and ride mankind."

If voluntary organizations, and stale and local governments, cannot find the imagination and energy necessary to meet our difficulties, probably we must fail to become a great society—indeed, ours may not remain a tolerable society. Even zealots for action on a national scale now confess that the nominal decision-makers in Washington have bitten off more than they can chew, and that the new responsibilities assumed by federal authorities during the past few years are almost impossible to administer.

Washington has no peculiar powers of creation: indeed, Washington is mostly a dormitory- town, without social or cultural continuity, administering much but originating little. The sources of creativity are elsewhere.

This commentator is lost in wonder at the ingenuousness of people who ought to know better—including a good many professors—concerning centralization and its consequences. These gentlemen assume that once all our affairs are thoroughly directed by the Executive Force in the nation's capital; we will march to Zion promptly.

But America has no tradition of central direction. Our moral and intellectual achievements, like our economic abundance, have been produced by individuals and groups scattered over the face of the land, not by patronage from a central source of benefaction. If our ceases to be a voluntary and diverse society, it loses its genius.

And here is what Barry Goldwater—another conservative icon—wrote about this very subject:

The currently favored instrument of collectivization is the Welfare State. The collectivists have not abandoned their ultimate goal—to subordinate the individual to the State—but their strategy has changed. They have learned that Socialism can be achieved through Welfarism quite as well as through Nationalization. They understand that private property can be put at the mercy of the State—not only by making the State his employer—but by divesting him of the means to provide for his personal needs and by giving the State the responsibility of caring for those needs from cradle to grave.

Moreover, they have discovered—and here is the critical point—that Welfarism is much more compatible with the political processes of a democratic society. Nationalization ran into popular opposition, but the collectivists feel sure the Welfare State can be erected by the simple expedient of buying votes with promises of "free" school aid, "free" hospitalization, "free" retirement pay and so on… The correctness of this estimate can be seen from the portion of the federal budget that is now allocated to welfare, an amount second only to the cost of national defense.

Yet, as it is well known, not all Conservatives think the same way on all issues. In fact, as neoconservative Irving Kristol put it,

The idea of a welfare state is perfectly consistent with a conservative political philosophy—as Bismarck knew, a hundred years ago. In our urbanized, industrialized, highly mobile society, people need governmental action of some kind if they are to cope with many of their problems: old age, illness, unemployment, etc. They need such assistance; they demand it; they will get it. The only interesting political question is: *How* will they get it?

But, he goes on, "this is not a question the Republican party has faced up to, because it still feels, deep down, that a welfare state is inconsistent with such traditional American virtues as self-reliance and individual liberty." Be it as it may, each of the factions of the American right—the fiscal conservative right, the social conservative right, the neoconservative right, the libertarian right, etc.— has proposed its own version of the "conservative" welfare state. According to political analyst and journalist Yuval Levin, for instance, conservatism's task is to shape the social insurance state, not repeal it:

The fact is that we do not face a choice between the liberal welfare state on one hand and austerity on the other. Those are two sides of the same coin: Austerity and decline are what will come if we do not reform the welfare state. The choice we face is between that combination and a different approach to balancing our society's deepest aspirations. America still has a little time to find such an alternative. Our moment of reckoning is coming, but it is not yet here. We have perhaps a decade in which to avert it and to foster again the preconditions for growth and opportunity without forcing a great disruption in the lives of millions, if we start now.

But we do not yet know quite how. The answer will not come from the left, which is far too committed to the old vision to accept its fate and contemplate alternatives. It must therefore emerge from the right. Conservatives must produce not only arguments against the liberal welfare state but also a different vision, a different answer to the question of how we might balance our aspirations. It must be a vision that emphasizes the pursuit of economic growth, republican virtues, and social mobility over economic security, value-neutral welfare, and material equality; that redefines the safety net as a means of making the poor more independent rather than making the middle class less so; and that translates these ideals into institutional forms that suit our modern, dynamic society.

That different vision is now beginning to take shape. Slowly, bit by bit, we are starting to see what must replace our welfare state.

1   Russell Kirk, "A Creative Society of the Future?" *The Herald Tribune*, Thursday, May 25, 1967.

2   Goldwater, *The Conscience of a Conservative*, pp. 63-64

3   Irving Kristol, *Neoconservatism: The Autobiography of an Idea: Selected Essays 1949-1995*, New York, N.Y.: The Free Press, 1995, p. 346.

4   Yuval Levin, "Beyond the Welfare State," *National Affairs*, #7, Spring 2011. www.nationalaffairs.com/doclib/20110317_Levin.pdf

24

X XENOPHOBIA

In his blog[1], conservative radio show host and columnist Dennis Prager maintains that the Left now smears Conservatives with SIXHIRB, his acronym for "Sexist, Intolerant, Xenophobic, Homophobic, Islamophobic, Racist, Bigoted."

But no true conservative can be xenophobic or racist, or anything like that. Rather, he is a critic of multiculturalism, but being anti-multiculturalism is virtually the same as being adverse to political correctness. Why? Because (modern) liberalism and leftism are religions…, and much water has passed under the bridge since liberals would corroborate the famous citation of Voltaire, "I do not agree with what you have to say, but I'll defend to the death your right to say it." Whilst claiming to support free speech, they show by their political actions and declarations an underlying desire to foster a veiled form of totalitarianism, a milder version of Stalinism based on crushing dissents and silencing opposition.

Here is an excerpt from. a speech[2] by British Prime

Minister David Cameron, in which he told a security conference in Germany that the UK needed to defend national identity to prevent extremism, and that "the doctrine of state multiculturalism" is a strategy which has "encouraged different cultures to live separate lives, apart from each other and apart from the mainstream."

Under the doctrine of state multiculturalism, we have encouraged different cultures to live separate lives, apart from each other and apart from the mainstream. We've failed to provide a vision of society to which they feel they want to belong. We've even tolerated these segregated communities behaving in ways that run completely counter to our values.

So, when a white person holds objectionable views, racist views for instance, we rightly condemn them. But when equally unacceptable views or practices come from someone who isn't white, we've been too cautious frankly—frankly, even fearful—to stand up to them. The failure, for instance, of some to confront the horrors of forced marriage, the practice where some young girls are bullied and sometimes taken abroad to marry someone when they don't want to, is a case in point. This hands-off tolerance has only served to reinforce the sense that not enough is shared. And this all leaves some young Muslims feeling rootless. And the search for something to belong to and something to believe in can lead them to this extremist ideology. Now for sure, they don't turn into terrorists overnight, but what we see—and what we see in so many European countries—is a process of radicalisation.

Internet chatrooms are virtual meeting places where attitudes are shared, strengthened and validated. In some mosques, preachers of hate can sow misinformation about the plight of Muslims elsewhere. In our communities, groups and organisations led by young, dynamic leaders promote separatism by encouraging Muslims to define themselves solely in terms of their religion. All these interactions can engender a sense of community, a substitute for what the wider society has failed to supply. Now, you might say, as long as they're not hurting anyone, what is the problem with all this?

Well, I'll tell you why. As evidence emerges about the backgrounds of those convicted of terrorist offences, it is clear that many of them were initially influenced by what some have called 'non-violent extremists', and they then took those radical beliefs to the next level by embracing violence. And I say this is an indictment of our approach to these issues in the past. And if we are to defeat this threat, I believe it is time to turn the page on the failed policies of the past. So first, instead of ignoring this extremist ideology, we—as governments and as societies—have got to confront it, in all its forms. And second, instead of encouraging people to live apart, we need a clear sense of shared national identity that is open to everyone.

1   The Dennis Prager Show : www.dennisprager.com/if-you-are-not-a-leftist-why-are-you-voting-democrat

2   British Prime Minister David Cameron's speech at Munich Security Conference (February 5, 2011): number10.gov.uk/news/pms-speech-at-Munich-security-conference

25

Y YOUTUBE

YouTube is becoming much more than an entertainment destination.

~*Chad Hurley* [1]

Well, before you accuse me of "jumping the shark" by wasting time writing about YouTube instead of about conservative issues, please heed this: has been established that YouTube is not only the world's biggest music streaming service, but also a valid source for both simple and in-depth historical research and analysis.

For instance, YouTube is the place where you can find excerpts from The History Channel's "The Presidents" series (featuring great conservatives such as George Washington, Thomas Jefferson, James Monroe, Abraham Lincoln, Theodore Roosevelt, etc.), or where you can relive many of the modern day historical moments, such as the most significant events of the Reagan era (including major speeches before national and international audiences, public appearances, etc.). How exhilarating it is to relive those moments, and what is more, this service is free and always available![2]

Now, we know that, by definition, unlike liberals, conservatives are not future-oriented, they are rather past-oriented and history absorbed. A very good reason why YouTube—a virtual bridge between the past and present—should not be underestimated by true conservatives! Then give unto Caesar what is Caesar's!

1   Chad Hurley is the co-founder and former CEO of the video-sharing website YouTube.com.
2   To get an idea watch Ronald Reagan's "A Time for Choosing," 1964, Televised Campaign Address for Goldwater presidential Campaign: http://youtu.be/qXBswFfh6AY (full text in Appendix 2 of this book). You can also have a quick look at www.youtube.com/user/PlanoProf/videoskkkk and www.youtube.com/watch?v=FSOE537LE4c&list=RDFSOE537LE4c.

26

Z ZEALOTS

Left-wing zealots have often been prepared to ride roughshod
over due process and basic considerations of fairness when they
think they can get away with it. For them the ends always seems
to justify the means. That is precisely how their predecessors
came to create the gulag.

~*Margaret Thatcher* [1]

A few lines before the above quoted passage, the Iron Lady
had written (speaking about the very same subject): "They
think that they are crusading for a better world. And that
conviction is precisely what makes them so dangerous."
Holy words, no question about that. But, one might object
that there are left-wing zealots as well as right-wing zealots
upon this earth! Well, this is true and it isn't, depending on
what is meant by "right-wing." If "right-wing"—as is
generally believed—is not a synonym of "conservative,"
then the objection is well founded, but if the two terms are
synonymous, then the objection is ill-founded. In other
words, no "true" conservative can be a zealot, and this for

the simple reason that conservatism, as we have already seen (in chapter 3), is neither an ideology nor a creed, nor a doctrine. And you cannot be a zealot without having any ideology, or creed, or doctrine, just as you cannot (politically) crusade—to paraphrase Margaret Thatcher's quote—if you don't believe a radically better world is achievable.

1   Margaret Thatcher, *Statecraft: Strategies for a Changing World*, New York, N.Y.: HarperCollins Publishers Inc., 2002, p. 273.

APPENDIX 1

KINDS OF CONSERVATISM
With Special Reference to the U.S.A.

CULTURAL CONSERVATISM

Cultural Conservatism supports preservation of the heritage of a nation or culture. Often confused with social conservatism, in the US the term may incorrectly describe members of the religious right, in fact the two share opinions on key social issues. The goal of cultural conservatives is to preserve and maintain the American way-of-life both at home and abroad.

SOCIAL CONSERVATISM

Unlike in Europe, where the expression usually refers to "Liberal" Conservatives, who support modern European welfare states, in the U.S. it refers to a moral school of thought based on family-values and religious (Judeo-Christian) traditions. Social conservatives hold firmly to a pro-life, pro-family and pro-religion agenda. They emphasize convention, morality and established roles within society and the family. In particular, they support traditional gender roles, marriage and "family values." The "pro-life" anti-abortion movement is an example of social conservatism in action. Social conservatives tend to strongly identify with American patriotism. They hold that military institutions embody core values such as honor, duty, courage, loyalty, commitment, integrity and selfless dedication. In recent years social conservatives played a major role in the political coalitions of Ronald Reagan and George W. Bush.

PALEOCONSERVATISM

Paleoconservatism (sometimes shortened to *paleocon*) stresses Judeo-Christian tradition and the importance to society of the traditional family. Paleoconservatives—a relatively small group of conservative intellectuals and commentators, often Catholics of Eastern European background—believe they are the true heirs to the U.S. conservative movement and are critical of other kinds of conservatism. Arguing that multiracial, multi-ethnic, and egalitarian states are inherently unstable, many of them call for strong restrictions on immigration and a rollback of multicultural programs. Classical liberals in many respects, Paleoconservatives emphasize economic nationalism and are generally isolationist in the conduct of American foreign policy—they have also reached out to libertarians who share their disdain for the "welfare-warfare state." The magazines *Chronicles* and *The American Conservative* are generally considered to be paleoconservative in nature. The most prominent figure is TV commentator and author Pat Buchanan.

NEOCONSERVATISM

Neoconservatism (sometimes shortened to *neocon*) is a modern form of conservatism that emerged in the U.S. in response to the perceived liberalism of the 1960s. Irving Kristol, co-founder of *Encounter* magazine, is largely credited with founding the neoconservative movement. He defined a *neoconservative* as "a liberal who was mugged by reality." Neoconservatism emphasizes free trade and free market economics, and an interventionist foreign policy aimed at promoting democracy abroad (many of the most prominent and influential conservatives during the two terms of the Bush administration were considered neoconservative in their ideological orientation). Neoconservatives hold a strong belief in social progress and the universality of human rights. They maintain that there is a universal desire to live in a technologically advanced and prosperous society and modern liberal democracies are one of the byproducts of such modernization.

THEOCONSERVATISM

This term (sometimes shortened to *theocon*) first appeared in 1996 in a *The New Republic* article entitled "Neocon v. Theocon" by Jacob Heilbrunn. "[T]he neoconservatives," wrote Heilbrunn, "believe that America is special because it was founded on an idea—a commitment to the rights of man embodied in the Declaration of Independence—not in ethnic or religious affiliations. The *theocons*, too, argue that America is rooted in an idea, but they believe that idea is Christianity." Aside from ridiculous comparisons between the theocons and the old throne-and-altar European right, a theoconservative is a person who holds the political philosophy that religion should play a role in forming public policy. The founder of the theocon movement is Richard John Neuhaus, a former Lutheran pastor who became Catholic in 1990 and a priest in 1991. Along with Neuhaus, the two most important theocons are Michael Novak and George Weigel, both of them Catholics. Both Fr. Neuhaus and Mr. Novak were radicals in the 1960s and early 1970s, both involved in protesting the Vietnam War. By the 1980s, both Neuhaus and Novak moved rightward. A biographer of Pope John Paul II, George Weigel has contributed to theocon ideas in the areas of American political thought and international relations. Weigel argues that American principles derive from medieval Catholic sources. At the same time he maintains that the country's political institutions require a religious foundation in order to maintain their vitality.

FISCAL CONSERVATISM

Fiscal Conservatism is the economic and political policy that advocates restraint of governmental taxation and expenditures. This economic philosophy of prudence in government spending and debt, is based on the principle that a government does not have the right to run up large debts and then throw the burden on the taxpayer. Fiscal conservatives support free market capitalism with minimal regulation and reject the Keynesian policy of deficit spending. They argue that big spending ruins the morals of the people, and that a national debt creates a dangerous class of speculators. Unlike in Europe, where many economic conservatives are not socially conservative, in the U.S. the two forms of conservatism are often—if not almost always—closely intertwined, especially within the Republican Party.

LIBERTARIAN CONSERVATISM

Libertarian conservatism (also known as conservative libertarianism) is a political philosophy that combines right-libertarian politics—leaning towards laissez-faire economics and a critical view of the federal government—and a belief in a more traditional, conservative social philosophy that stresses the importance of authority and duty. Frank Meyer, a co-founder of *National Review,* has called this combination fusionism. Paleolibertarianism (closely associated with the Austrian School of economics, paleolibertarians identify as anarcho-capitalist), Constitutionalism (which advocates the maximization of civil and economic liberties) and neolibertarianism (which advocates maximizing civil liberties while upholding national security objectives) consist as the branches of libertarian conservatism. Libertarian conservatives may be more militarily interventionist than other libertarians—there is a long history of libertarian-conservatives rejecting non-interventionist foreign policy (for instance, during the Vietnam War, Barry Goldwater advocated regime change in North Vietnam).

REAGAN CONSERVATISM

Reagan's conservative philosophy was rooted in the famous "City upon a Hill" sermon (1630) by John Winthrop. Those words—*"For wee must consider that wee shall be as a citty upon a hill, the eies of all people are uppon us"*—defined Reagan's vision, and version, of conservatism and of America. Speaking at his alma mater, Eureka College, in 1957, he stated:

> Looming large in your inheritance is this country, this land America, placed as it is between two great oceans. Those who discovered and pioneered it had to have rare qualities of courage and imagination nor did these qualities stop there. Even the modern-day immigrants have been possessed of courage beyond that of their neighbors. The courage to tear up centuries-old roots and leave their homelands, to come to this land where even the language was strange. Such courage is part of our inheritance, all of us spring from these special people and these qualities have contributed to the make-up of the American personality.

In his newest book, *11 Principles of a Reagan Conservative*, Reagan biographer Paul Kengor has set out the core tenets of those who call themselves Reagan conservatives:

1. Freedom
2. Faith
3. Family
4. Sanctity and Dignity of Human Life
5. American Exceptionalism
6. The Founders' Wisdom and Vision
7. Lower Taxes
8. Limited Government
9. Peace Through Strength
10. Anti-Communism
11. Belief in the Individual

At the end of his book Kengor writes:

> So, when hearing a Republican presidential aspirant invoking the name of Ronald Reagan, consider whether the candidate shares Reagan's faith-based optimism, his belief in the individual, his belief in American exceptionalism, his regard for the sanctity and dignity of unborn human life. Is the candidate the pessimist in the room full of toys or the optimist searching for the pony in the dung heap? Would the candidate submit the "foundational" and "divine institution" of the family to the harm of the latest cultural trend, dictate, fad, or fashion? If you hear a self-professing conservative heralding "freedom," ask whether he or she believes that a self-governing nation can govern freely without the vital moral rudder that is faith. Can there be genuine freedom without faith? What did Tocqueville say? Reagan said what Tocqueville said.
>
> This, and more, is what a Reagan conservative would say.
>
> And finally, Reagan's conservatism […] was also an affirmation of his personal idea of America and what it means to be an American. Reagan said that America is less of a place than an idea. […] Understanding Reagan's conservatism also means understanding Reagan's very concept of the idea of America. Really, then, to answer the question "What is a Reagan conservative?" is less a particular political lesson than an enduring civics lesson. It has value for all American citizens going forward.

CRUNCHY CONSERVATISM

This term was coined by *National Review* commentator Rod Dreher in 2006, when he published a book titled *Crunchy Cons*, with the subtitle being, *How Birkenstocked Burkeans, gun-loving organic gardeners, evangelical free-range farmers, hip homeschooling mamas, right wing nature lovers, and their diverse tribe of countercultural conservatives plan to save America (or at least the Republican Party)*. And that's how the crunchy conservative movement began. Crunchy conservatives, says Dreher, are conservatives "who stand outside the conservative mainstream." United by a "cultural sensibility, not an ideology," crunchy conservatives, he says, have some habits and beliefs often identified with cultural liberals. For instance, they patronize small business such as organic food stores and markets, and recycle as if the world depended on it. To crunchy cons, the world *does* depend on it. Dreher describes crunchy cons as those "who embrace a counter-cultural, yet traditional conservative lifestyle." They tend to focus more on family-oriented, culturally conservative concepts such as being good stewards of the natural world and avoiding materialism in everyday life. The book includes the following ten-point "Crunchy Cons Manifesto":

1. We are conservatives who stand outside the conservative mainstream; therefore, we can see things that matter more clearly.
2. Modern conservatism has become too focused on money, power, and the accumulation of stuff, and insufficiently concerned with the content of our individual and social character.
3. Big business deserves as much skepticism as big government.
4. Culture is more important than politics and economics.
5. A conservatism that does not practice restraint, humility, and good stewardship—especially of the natural world—is not fundamentally conservative.
6. Small, Local, Old, and Particular are almost always better than Big, Global, New, and Abstract.
7. Beauty is more important than efficiency.
8. The relentlessness of media-driven pop culture deadens our senses to authentic truth, beauty, and wisdom.
9. We share Russell Kirk's conviction that "the institution most essential to conserve is the family."
10. Politics and economics won't save us; if our culture is to be saved at all, it will be by faithfully living by the Permanent Things, conserving these ancient moral truths in the choices we make in our everyday lives.

APPENDIX 2

A TIME FOR CHOOSING
(also known as "The Speech")

By Ronald Reagan
October 27, 1964
Televised Campaign Address for Goldwater presidential Campaign

Thank you. Thank you very much. Thank you and good evening. The sponsor has been identified, but unlike most television programs, the performer hasn't been provided with a script. As a matter of fact, I have been permitted to choose my own words and discuss my own ideas regarding the choice that we face in the next few weeks.

I have spent most of my life as a Democrat. I recently have seen fit to follow another course. I believe that the issues confronting us cross party lines. Now, one side in this campaign has been telling us that the issues of this election are the maintenance of peace and prosperity. The line has been used, "We've never had it so good."

But I have an uncomfortable feeling that this prosperity isn't something on which we can base our hopes for the future. No nation in history has ever survived a tax burden that reached a third of its national income. Today, 37 cents out of every dollar earned in this country is the tax collector's share, and yet our government continues to spend 17 million dollars a day more than the government takes in. We haven't balanced our budget 28 out of the last 34 years. We've raised our debt limit three times in the last twelve months, and now our national debt is one and a half times bigger than all the combined debts of all the nations of the world. We have 15 billion dollars in gold in our treasury; we don't own an ounce. Foreign dollar claims are 27.3 billion dollars. And we've just had announced that the dollar of 1939 will now purchase 45 cents in its total value.

As for the peace that we would preserve, I wonder who among us would like to approach the wife or mother whose husband or son has died in South Vietnam and ask them if they think this is a peace that should be maintained indefinitely. Do they mean peace, or do they mean we just want to be left in peace? There can be no real peace while one American is dying some place in the world for the rest of us. We're at war with the most dangerous enemy that has ever faced mankind in his long climb from the swamp to the stars, and it's been said if we lose that war, and in so doing lose this way of freedom of ours, history will record with the greatest astonishment that those who had the most to lose did the least to prevent its happening. Well I think it's time we ask ourselves if we still know the freedoms that were intended for us by the Founding Fathers.

Not too long ago, two friends of mine were talking to a Cuban refugee, a businessman who had escaped from Castro, and in the midst of his story one of my friends turned to the other and said, "We don't know how lucky we are." And the Cuban stopped and said, "How lucky you are? I had someplace to escape to." And in that sentence he told us the entire story. If we lose freedom here, there's no place to escape to. This is the last stand on earth.

And this idea that government is beholden to the people, that it has no other source of power except the sovereign people, is still the newest and the most unique idea in all the long history of man's relation to man.

This is the issue of this election: Whether we believe in our capacity for self-government or whether we abandon the American revolution and confess that a little intellectual elite in a far-distant capitol can plan our lives for us better than we can plan them ourselves.

You and I are told increasingly we have to choose between a left or right. Well I'd like to suggest there is no such thing as a left or right. There's only an up or down—[up] man's old—old-aged dream, the ultimate in individual freedom consistent with law and order, or down to the ant heap of totalitarianism. And regardless of their sincerity, their humanitarian motives, those who would trade our freedom for security have embarked on this downward course.

In this vote-harvesting time, they use terms like the "Great Society," or as we were told a few days ago by the President, we must accept a greater government activity in the affairs of the people. But they've been a little more explicit in the past and among themselves; and all of the things I now will quote have appeared in print. These are not Republican accusations. For example, they have voices that say, "The cold war will end through our acceptance of a not undemocratic socialism." Another voice says, "The profit motive has become outmoded. It must be replaced by the incentives of the welfare state." Or, "Our traditional system of individual freedom is incapable of solving the complex problems of the 20th century." Senator Fullbright has said at Stanford University that the Constitution is outmoded. He referred to the President as "our moral teacher and our leader," and he says he is "hobbled in his task by the restrictions of power imposed on him by this antiquated document." He must "be freed," so that he "can do for us" what he knows "is best." And Senator Clark of Pennsylvania, another articulate spokesman, defines liberalism as "meeting the material needs of the masses through the full power of centralized government."

Well, I, for one, resent it when a representative of the people refers to you and me, the free men and women of this country, as "the masses." This is a term we haven't applied to ourselves in America. But beyond that, "the full power of centralized government"—this was the very thing the Founding Fathers sought to minimize. They knew that governments don't control things. A government can't control the economy without controlling people. And they know when a government sets out to do that, it must use force and coercion to achieve its purpose. They also knew, those Founding Fathers, that outside of its legitimate functions, government does nothing as well or as economically as the private sector of the economy.

Now, we have no better example of this than government's involvement in the farm economy over the last 30 years. Since 1955, the cost of this program has nearly doubled. One-fourth of farming in America is responsible for 85 percent of the farm surplus. Three-fourths of farming is out on the free market and has known a 21 percent increase in the per capita consumption of all its produce. You see, that one-fourth of farming—that's regulated and controlled by the federal government. In the last three years we've spent 43 dollars in the feed grain program for every dollar bushel of corn we don't grow.

Senator Humphrey last week charged that Barry Goldwater, as President, would seek to eliminate farmers. He should do his homework a little better, because he'll find out that we've had a decline of 5 million in the farm population under these government programs. He'll also find that the Democratic administration has sought to get from Congress [an] extension of the farm program to include that three-fourths that is now free. He'll find that they've also asked for the right to imprison farmers who wouldn't keep books as prescribed by the federal government. The Secretary of Agriculture asked for the right to seize farms through condemnation and resell them to other individuals. And contained in that same program was a provision that would have allowed the federal government to remove 2 million farmers from the soil.

At the same time, there's been an increase in the Department of Agriculture employees. There's now one for every 30 farms in the United States, and still they can't tell us how 66 shiploads of grain headed for Austria disappeared without a trace and Billie Sol Estes never left shore.

Every responsible farmer and farm organization has repeatedly asked the government to free the farm economy, but how—who are farmers to know what's best for them? The wheat farmers voted against a wheat program. The government passed it anyway. Now the price of bread goes up; the price of wheat to the farmer goes down.

Meanwhile, back in the city, under urban renewal the assault on freedom carries on. Private property rights [are] so diluted that public interest is almost anything a few government planners decide it should be. In a program that takes from the needy and gives to the greedy, we see such spectacles as in Cleveland, Ohio, a million-and-a-half-dollar building completed only three years ago must be destroyed to make way for what government officials call a "more compatible use of the land." The President tells us he's now going to start building public housing units in the thousands, where heretofore we've only built them in the hundreds. But FHA [Federal Housing Authority] and the Veterans Administration tell us they have 120,000 housing units they've taken back through mortgage foreclosure. For three decades, we've sought to solve the problems of unemployment through government planning, and the more the plans fail, the more the planners plan. The latest is the Area Redevelopment Agency.

They've just declared Rice County, Kansas, a depressed area. Rice County, Kansas, has two hundred oil wells, and the 14,000 people there have over 30 million dollars on deposit in personal savings in their banks. And when the government tells you you're depressed, lie down and be depressed.

We have so many people who can't see a fat man standing beside a thin one without coming to the conclusion the fat man got that way by taking advantage of the thin one. So they're going to solve all the problems of human misery through government and government planning. Well, now, if government planning and welfare had the answer—and they've had almost 30 years of it—shouldn't we expect government to read the score to us once in a while? Shouldn't they be telling us about the decline each year in the number of people needing help? The reduction in the need for public housing?

But the reverse is true. Each year the need grows greater; the program grows greater. We were told four years ago that 17 million people went to bed hungry each night. Well that was probably true. They were all on a diet. But now we're told that 9.3 million families in this country are poverty-stricken on the basis of earning less than 3,000 dollars a year. Welfare spending [is] 10 times greater than in the dark depths of the Depression. We're spending 45 billion dollars on welfare. Now do a little arithmetic, and you'll find that if we divided the 45 billion dollars up equally among those 9 million poor families, we'd be able to give each family 4,600 dollars a year. And this added to their present income should eliminate poverty. Direct aid to the poor, however, is only running only about 600 dollars per family. It would seem that someplace there must be some overhead.

Now—so now we declare "war on poverty," or "You, too, can be a Bobby Baker." Now do they honestly expect us to believe that if we add 1 billion dollars to the 45 billion we're spending, one more program to the 30-odd we have—and remember, this new program doesn't replace any, it just duplicates existing programs—do they believe that poverty is suddenly going to disappear by magic? Well, in all fairness I should explain there is one part of the new program that isn't duplicated. This is the youth feature. We're now going to solve the dropout problem, juvenile delinquency, by reinstituting something like the old CCC camps [Civilian Conservation Corps], and we're going to put our young people in these camps. But again we do some arithmetic, and we find that we're going to spend each year just on room and board for each young person we help 4,700 dollars a year. We can send them to Harvard for 2,700! Course, don't get me wrong. I'm not suggesting Harvard is the answer to juvenile delinquency.

But seriously, what are we doing to those we seek to help? Not too long ago, a judge called me here in Los Angeles. He told me of a young woman who'd come before him for a divorce. She had six children, was pregnant with her seventh. Under his questioning, she revealed her husband was a laborer earning 250 dollars a month. She wanted a divorce to get an 80 dollar raise. She's eligible for 330 dollars a month in the Aid to Dependent Children Program. She got the idea from two women in her neighborhood who'd already done that very thing.

Yet anytime you and I question the schemes of the do-gooders, we're denounced as being against their humanitarian goals. They say we're always "against" things—we're never "for" anything.

Well, the trouble with our liberal friends is not that they're ignorant; it's just that they know so much that isn't so.

Now—we're for a provision that destitution should not follow unemployment by reason of old age, and to that end we've accepted Social Security as a step toward meeting the problem.

But we're against those entrusted with this program when they practice deception regarding its fiscal shortcomings, when they charge that any criticism of the program means that we want to end payments to those people who depend on them for a livelihood. They've called it "insurance" to us in a hundred million pieces of literature. But then they appeared before the Supreme Court and they testified it was a welfare program. They only use the term "insurance" to sell it to the people. And they said Social Security dues are a tax for the general use of the government, and the government has used that tax. There is no fund, because Robert Byers, the actuarial head, appeared before a congressional committee and admitted that Social Security as of this moment is 298 billion dollars in the hole. But he said there should be no cause for worry because as long as they have the power to tax, they could always take away from the people whatever they needed to bail them out of trouble. And they're doing just that.

A young man, 21 years of age, working at an average salary—his Social Security contribution would, in the open market, buy him an insurance policy that would guarantee 220 dollars a month at age 65. The government promises 127. He could live it up until he's 31 and then take out a policy that would pay more than Social Security. Now are we so lacking in business sense that we can't put this program on a sound basis, so that people who do require those payments will find they can get them when they're due—that the cupboard isn't bare? Barry Goldwater thinks we can.

At the same time, can't we introduce voluntary features that would permit a citizen who can do better on his own to be excused upon presentation of evidence that he had made provision for the non-earning years? Should we not allow a widow with children to work, and not lose the benefits supposedly paid for by her deceased husband? Shouldn't you and I be allowed to declare who our beneficiaries will be under this program, which we cannot do? I think we're for telling our senior citizens that no one in this country should be denied medical care because of a lack of funds. But I think we're against forcing all citizens, regardless of need, into a compulsory government program, especially when we have such examples, as was announced last week, when France admitted that their Medicare program is now bankrupt. They've come to the end of the road.

In addition, was Barry Goldwater so irresponsible when he suggested that our government give up its program of deliberate, planned inflation, so that when you do get your Social Security pension, a dollar will buy a dollar's worth, and not 45 cents worth?

I think we're for an international organization, where the nations of the world can seek peace. But I think we're against subordinating American interests to an organization that has become so structurally unsound that today you can muster a two-thirds vote on the floor of the General Assembly among nations that represent less than 10 percent of the world's population. I think we're against the hypocrisy of assailing our allies because here and there they cling to a colony, while we engage in a conspiracy of silence and never open our mouths about the millions of people enslaved in the Soviet colonies in the satellite nations.

I think we're for aiding our allies by sharing of our material blessings with those nations which share in our fundamental beliefs, but we're against doling out money government to government, creating bureaucracy, if not socialism, all over the world. We set out to help 19 countries. We're helping 107. We've spent 146 billion dollars. With that money, we bought a 2 million dollar yacht for Haile Selassie. We bought dress suits for Greek undertakers, extra wives for Kenya[n] government officials. We bought a thousand TV sets for a place where they have no electricity. In the last six years, 52 nations have bought 7 billion dollars worth of our gold, and all 52 are receiving foreign aid from this country.

No government ever voluntarily reduces itself in size. So governments'programs, once launched, never disappear.

Actually, a government bureau is the nearest thing to eternal life we'll ever see on this earth.

Federal employees—federal employees number two and a half million; and federal, state, and local, one out of six of the nation's work force employed by government. These proliferating bureaus with their thousands of regulations have cost us many of our constitutional safeguards. How many of us realize that today federal agents can invade a man's property without a warrant? They can impose a fine without a formal hearing, let alone a trial by jury? And they can seize and sell his property at auction to enforce the payment of that fine. In Chico County, Arkansas, James Wier over-planted his rice allotment. The government obtained a 17,000 dollar judgment. And a U.S. marshal sold his 960-acre farm at auction. The government said it was necessary as a warning to others to make the system work.

Last February 19th at the University of Minnesota, Norman Thomas, six-times candidate for President on the Socialist Party ticket, said, "If Barry Goldwater became President, he would stop the advance of socialism in the United States." I think that's exactly what he will do.
　　But as a former Democrat, I can tell you Norman Thomas isn't the only man who has drawn this parallel to socialism with the present administration, because back in 1936, Mr. Democrat himself, Al Smith, the great American, came before the American people and charged that the leadership of his Party was taking the Party of Jefferson, Jackson, and Cleveland down the road under the banners of Marx, Lenin, and Stalin. And he walked away from his Party, and he never returned til the day he died—because to this day, the

leadership of that Party has been taking that Party, that honorable Party, down the road in the image of the labor Socialist Party of England.

Now it doesn't require expropriation or confiscation of private property or business to impose socialism on a people. What does it mean whether you hold the deed to the—or the title to your business or property if the government holds the power of life and death over that business or property? And such machinery already exists. The government can find some charge to bring against any concern it chooses to prosecute. Every businessman has his own tale of harassment. Somewhere a perversion has taken place. Our natural, unalienable rights are now considered to be a dispensation of government, and freedom has never been so fragile, so close to slipping from our grasp as it is at this moment.

Our Democratic opponents seem unwilling to debate these issues. They want to make you and I believe that this is a contest between two men—that we're to choose just between two personalities.

Well what of this man that they would destroy—and in destroying, they would destroy that which he represents, the ideas that you and I hold dear? Is he the brash and shallow and trigger-happy man they say he is? Well I've been privileged to know him "when." I knew him long before he ever dreamed of trying for high office, and I can tell you personally I've never known a man in my life I believed so incapable of doing a dishonest or dishonorable thing.

This is a man who, in his own business before he entered politics, instituted a profit-sharing plan before unions had ever thought of it. He put in health and medical insurance for all his employees. He took 50 percent of the profits before taxes and set up a retirement program, a pension plan for all his employees. He sent monthly checks for life to an employee who was ill and couldn't work. He provides nursing care for the children of mothers who work in the stores. When Mexico was ravaged by the floods in the Rio Grande, he climbed in his airplane and flew medicine and supplies down there.

An ex-GI told me how he met him. It was the week before Christmas during the Korean War, and he was at the Los Angeles airport trying to get a ride home to Arizona for Christmas. And he said that [there were] a lot of servicemen there and no seats available on the planes. And then a voice came over the loudspeaker and said, "Any men in uniform wanting a ride to Arizona, go to runway such-and-such," and they went down there, and there was a fellow named Barry Goldwater sitting in his plane. Every day in those weeks before Christmas, all day long, he'd load up the plane, fly it to Arizona, fly them to their homes, fly back over to get another load.

During the hectic split-second timing of a campaign, this is a man who took time out to sit beside an old friend who was dying of cancer. His campaign managers were understandably impatient, but he said, "There aren't many left who care what happens to her. I'd like her to know I care." This is a man who said to his 19-year-old son, "There is no foundation like the rock of honesty and fairness, and when you begin to build your life on that rock, with the cement of the faith in God that you have, then you have a real start." This is not a man who could carelessly send other people's sons to war. And that is the issue of this campaign that makes all the other problems I've discussed academic, unless we realize we're in a war that must be won.

Those who would trade our freedom for the soup kitchen of the welfare state have told us they have a utopian solution of peace without victory. They call their policy "accommodation." And they say if we'll only avoid any direct confrontation with the enemy, he'll forget his evil ways and learn to love us. All who oppose them are indicted as warmongers. They say we offer simple answers to complex problems. Well, perhaps there is a simple answer—not an easy answer—but simple: If you and I have the courage to tell our elected officials that we want our national policy based on what we know in our hearts is morally right.

We cannot buy our security, our freedom from the threat of the bomb by committing an immorality so great as saying to a billion human beings now enslaved behind the Iron Curtain, "Give up your dreams of freedom because to save our own skins, we're willing to make a deal with your slave masters." Alexander Hamilton said, "A nation which can prefer disgrace to danger is prepared for a master, and deserves one." Now let's set the record straight. There's no argument over the choice between peace and war, but there's only one guaranteed way you can have peace—and you can have it in the next second—surrender.

Admittedly, there's a risk in any course we follow other than this, but every lesson of history tells us that the greater risk lies in appeasement, and this is the specter our well-meaning liberal friends refuse to face—that their policy of accommodation is appeasement, and it gives no choice between peace and war, only between fight or surrender. If we continue to accommodate, continue to back and retreat, eventually we have to face the final demand—the ultimatum. And what then—when Nikita Khrushchev has told his people he knows what our answer will be? He has told them that we're retreating under the pressure of the Cold War, and someday when the time comes to deliver the final ultimatum, our surrender will be voluntary, because by that time we will have been weakened from within spiritually, morally, and economically. He believes this because from our side he's heard voices pleading for "peace at any price" or "better Red than dead," or as one commentator put it, he'd rather "live on his knees than die on his feet." And therein lies the road to war, because those voices don't speak for the rest of us.

You and I know and do not believe that life is so dear and peace so sweet as to be purchased at the price of chains and slavery. If nothing in life is worth dying for, when did this begin—just in the face of this enemy? Or should Moses have told the children of Israel to live in slavery under the pharaohs? Should Christ have refused the cross? Should the patriots at Concord Bridge have thrown down their guns and refused to fire the shot heard 'round the world? The martyrs of history were not fools, and our honored dead who gave their lives to stop the advance of the Nazis didn't die in vain. Where, then, is the road to peace? Well it's a simple answer after all.

You and I have the courage to say to our enemies, "There is a price we will not pay." "There is a point beyond which they must not advance." And this—this is the meaning in the phrase of Barry Goldwater's "peace through strength." Winston Churchill said, "The destiny of man is not measured by material computations. When great forces are on the move in the world, we learn we're spirits—not animals." And he said, "There's something going on in time and space, and beyond time and space, which, whether we like it or not, spells duty."

You and I have a rendezvous with destiny. We'll preserve for our children this, the last best hope of man on earth, or we'll sentence them to take the last step into a thousand years of darkness.

We will keep in mind and remember that Barry Goldwater has faith in us. He has faith that you and I have the ability and the dignity and the right to make our own decisions and determine our own destiny.

Thank you very much.

ABOUT THE AUTHOR

S.R. Piccoli (the initials stand for Samuele Roberto), aka Rob, was born the 13th November, 1950 on the Island of Maddalena—one of the most beautiful islands in the Mediterranean—off the northeast coast of Sardinia.

But his origins are nuanced. His mother was born in Philadelphia, although her family was originally from Liguria in northwest Italy, and his father was from Treviso in the northeast.

When he was very young his family moved to Rome, where he first went to school. After attending Classical High School, he studied political science for two years at the University of Rome. He then moved to Treviso (Venice Area), where he eventually settled.

From 1972 to 1975 Rob attended the University of Venice, where he graduated in philosophy. He also studied English at San Francisco State University in 1980.

Rob has been a High School teacher almost all his working life. Now that he has retired, he can finally spend more time doing what he loves most: writing.

Thomas Jefferson once said that, "every man has two countries—his own and France." Today, one could advance that, every man has two countries—his own and America. This is certainly the case with the author of this book. In his Twitter profile he describes himself, "European by birth, American by philosophy," which after all is quite an accurate description. Perhaps it also supports the adage that brevity is the soul of wit.

He lives with his wife, Clara, his daughter, Benedetta, and their dog, Lady, a golden retriever that swims like a fish and is crazy about tennis balls.

CONTACTS

rob.weblog@gmail.com
www.facebook.com/rpiccoli
twitter.com/robpiccoli
www.windrosehotel.com (blog)